MAHALO

A DAILY GRATITUDE JOURNAL

2018

TIMBER HAWKEYE

BUDDHISTBOOTCAMP.COM

HP

Hawkeye Publishers

Mahalo: A Daily Gratitude Journal 2018

No part of this publication may be used or reproduced in any manner whatsoever without written permission, except in the case of brief quotations embodied in critical articles and reviews.

© Copyright 2017 Hawkeye Publishers

For more information, address Hawkeye Publishers, P.O. Box 3098, Camarillo, CA 93011.

ISBN: 978-1946005618

HAWKEYEPUBLISHERS.COM

This gratitude journal belongs to

_____

KEEP
CALM
AND
THAT'S ALL..
JUST KEEP CALM

BUDDHISTBOOTCAMP.COM

Why is gratitude so important?

If you wake up each morning thinking you didn't get enough sleep the night before, or that perhaps you're not pretty enough, rich enough, successful enough, healthy enough, or anything-else-enough, it means you begin each day with the mindset of scarcity, and experience every moment from a place of lack. **But that's about to change!**

We are creatures of habit, and by actually using this gratitude journal every single morning, you will experience an all new and much healthier habit of focusing on abundance. Within two weeks you will start enjoying the richness of your life instead of always zooming-in on what's missing.

Consider this journal your companion, asking you each morning how well you slept the night before, checking-in on how you're feeling, and inviting you to share what you're most excited about.

Each day starts with the question, "How do you feel right now?" And since we tend to over-think things, you are reminded to pick only two words that best describe your current state of being. From inspired to exhausted, to feeling well-rested, optimistic, calm, or curious. There is no "wrong answer" here because this is just an initial scan to bring your awareness to the present moment.

_____Determined_____ 🔥 _____Optimistic_____

If you're not sure what you're feeling because there is too much going on in your life (or maybe not very much at all), here is a short list of a few possibilities to help you decide along the way.

You might be feeling confident, joyous, frisky, interested, loved, enthusiastic, receptive, daring, rebellious, lucky, overjoyed, liberated, comfortable, content, blessed, tender, fascinated, brave, daring, tenacious, certain or uncertain, irritable, sore, annoyed, resentful, tired, sulky, ashamed, hesitant, doubtful, lost, scared, desperate, offended, heartbroken, restless, or just bored and nonchalant. The possibilities are endless. Just keep in mind that you have a choice. You can either feel rejected or re-directed, for example; the switch in perspective might be difficult and foreign at first, but choosing happiness will become natural and second-nature by the end of the year.

Next you are asked to write down what you're grateful for, and there is a two-line limit to your answer because you would otherwise keep writing for hours. You might wake up grateful for a warm bed and a roof over your head one morning, and another day feel most grateful for a pair of functioning lungs or a wonderful job, or maybe a car, paved roads, bike lanes, sidewalks, or airplanes. There is no end to what we can appreciate because our lives are filled with so many gifts; from food to smart phones, friends, eyesight, limbs, sunshine, flip flops, rain, sweats, music, silence, children, or the lack thereof. Maybe you're grateful to be married or beyond grateful for divorce lawyers; there is no "wrong answer" here either. The important thing is to be grateful.

After those first two questions, which you will be asked every single morning: 1. How do you feel right now, and 2. What are you grateful for, each remaining day of the week presents three additional questions that differ from Monday through Sunday.

There is a reason behind every question in this journal, but each is either intended to enrich your own life or the lives of others (which, by default, improves your own as well). From inviting you to introduce a new healthy habit each week (be it parking farther from entrances so you can walk more, or drinking water instead of soda; it's up to you), and even sending one letter a week to a friend you haven't spoken to in a while. Don't over-think the letter or expect a response. Just say hello and a quick update about what's going well in your life, maybe a song, book, or movie recommendation that recently left an impression on you. Just imagine the smile on your friends' faces when they receive it!

Asking you what you can learn from current challenges in your life is a way of shifting your perspective from thinking that things happen TO you (which keeps you identifying as a victim), to realizing that everything happens FOR you (for you to learn from, grow from, and move on from), which keeps you searching for lessons instead of someone to blame.

Remember the last time you had the flu and could barely breathe? That's the reason behind seemingly silly questions like "What physical ability are you grateful for today?" It is designed to make you appreciate something as easily overlooked as breathing through your nose, which we often take for granted until the moment we can't do it.

Things you can do more-of can include anything from eating healthier to calling your mother, while things you can do less-of can include keeping quiet instead of arguing, and perhaps unsubscribing from some of those catalogs you keep getting in the mail.

Appreciating modern technology is an important reminder that some people don't have running water or electricity in their homes, let alone WiFi and Bluetooth. And asking you what you can do to relax is intended to inspire self-care, which we often overlook when we're constantly busy taking care of everyone else. So whether you choose to get a massage or simply unplug for thirty minutes and sit in silence, what you do to relax is up to you. The important thing is that you know how to do it (you'd be surprised how many people don't know how to answer this question).

Asking "What is your priority today?" is important because our actions truly convey our priorities. So even though you might be tempted to say, "My health is my priority," when you stay up until 2am to binge watch a new show even though your first appointment the next day is at 7am, it proves that your health isn't your priority after all. So a good answer to "What is your priority today?" could be "To sleep by 10pm" for example, or "To respond to all of my personal emails today so my inbox is finally empty instead of overflowing with unread messages."

Be sure you understand the difference between making an observation and making a judgment. There is nothing wrong with binge watching a new show. It may, in fact, be someone's priority for the day or their way to relax. The key is to live in congruence: to say what we mean and mean what we say. This journal is for you and you alone, so only you can hold yourself accountable. There is no judgment here, just an invitation to thrive.

Other questions remind you of your skills so you don't forget your worth, or the questions bring a different relationship into the spotlight each week so you never take it for granted. Hopefully your answer to "What piece of wisdom are you grateful for?" will be different each week. And good deeds we can do in secret are as simple as $10 anonymous donations to a non-profit organization online. Again, don't over-think these, they are intended to keep your momentum in a positive direction and on a path to grateful living (hence questions like "What freedoms do you take for granted" and "What goal did you accomplish this week or are closer to reaching?").

Each week I also invite you to contemplate how you are exactly the same as everyone else. I personally think it's the most important question in this journal because it connects all of us on the most basic, human level instead of segregating us by color, race, tax bracket, gender, religion, or geographical region. Remembering how we are all the same is the key to unlock your unwavering compassion for all living beings. This one question breaks down the illusion of "us" and "them," and shifts our perspective from a world of "me" to "we."

Psychologically speaking, gratitude is also a wonderful antidote to almost any negative feeling. You can't be angry and grateful at the same time, for example; it's not cognitively possible. Let's say you are angry with your spouse for a moment. It is only possible because you have momentarily forgotten how grateful you are to have them in your life. And the moment you go back to being grateful, the anger goes away. That's because gratitude keeps things in perspective while anger blows them out of proportion.

We start the year by writing down anything from previous years that we do not want to carry with us into 2018. This includes insecurities, negative self-talk, grudges, resentments, prejudices, fears, judgments, outdated opinions, and beliefs, but it can also be certain relationships or tangible items that take up space in your life. Liberate yourself by letting it go and starting the new year lighter than ever before.

Mahatma Gandhi said that happiness is the result of what we think, what we say, and what we do, all being in harmony. Only when we live in alignment with our core values does true happiness arise. It sounds simple enough, but it's actually impossible for us to live in line with our values if we're not clear about what those core values actually are. This is why I frequently invite you to write them down. There is space in the back of this book for you to detail your core values and write a paragraph or two describing the kind of life you want to lead. What kind of person do you want to be? After writing it all down, cross-reference it with the life you're currently living, and you'll see where you have some work to do. What's wonderful and empowering about this exercise is that nobody else is telling you what to do or how to be, you are inviting yourself to be the best version of you there is.

And just like we can't live in line with our values if we're not clear about what they are, many of us live a life of scarcity (of "not enough") because we haven't yet taken the time to define what "enough" looks like. If we don't know what "enough" is, we will never have it.

That's why gratitude is so important: it turns what we already have into "enough." And **that** is the true definition of luxury; **that** is being rich!

When you approach each moment with gratitude, not only will you stop experiencing life from a place of lack, you will experience abundance!

Mahalo nui loa (thank you very much),
from your brother,
Timber Hawkeye.

Reflections

List anything from last year that you do not want to carry with you into 2018 (be it grudges, outdated opinions, judgments, or beliefs that no longer serve your evolution). Then write down your intentions for 2018, and periodically visit this page to check on your progress.

_____

_____

_____

_____

_____

_____

_____

_____

Monday, January 1, 2018

In two words, how do you feel right now?

_____

What are you grateful for today?

_____

_____

What are you looking forward to today?

_____

_____

A healthy habit you can start as of right now:

_____

_____

A friend you can send a letter to today:

_____

Tuesday, January 2, 2018

In two words, how do you feel right now?

_____   _____

What are you grateful for today?

_____

_____

What can you learn from current challenges?

_____

_____

How can you make today awesome?

_____

_____

What physical ability are you grateful for today?

_____

Wednesday, January 3, 2018

In two words, how do you feel right now?

_____ _____

What are you grateful for today?

_____

_____

What would you like to do more often?

_____

_____

What would you like to do less often?

_____

_____

Modern technology you appreciate today:

_____

Thursday, January 4, 2018

In two words, how do you feel right now?

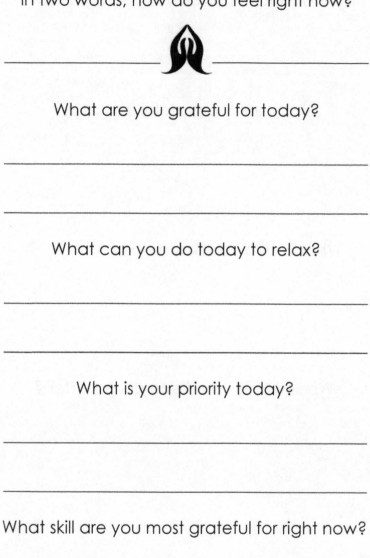

_____   _____

What are you grateful for today?

_____

_____

What can you do today to relax?

_____

_____

What is your priority today?

_____

_____

What skill are you most grateful for right now?

_____

Friday, January 5, 2018

In two words, how do you feel right now?

_____   _____

What are you grateful for today?

_____

_____

What do you have plenty of?

_____

_____

What piece of wisdom are you grateful for?

_____

_____

Which current relationship are you grateful for?

_____

Saturday, January 6, 2018

In two words, how do you feel right now?

_____   _____

What are you grateful for today?

_____

_____

What freedoms are you taking for granted?

_____

_____

From where do you gain your sense of self-worth?

_____

_____

What good deed can you do in secret today?

_____

Sunday, January 7, 2018

In two words, how do you feel right now?

_____ _____

What are you grateful for today?

_____

_____

A goal you can accomplish today or get closer to:

_____

_____

What happened this week you want to remember:

_____

_____

How are you exactly the same as everyone else?

_____

Reflections

Note the highlights in your life in this moment.
Write down a quote that motivates you,
the titles of books you want to read
or documentaries to watch,
and a reason to smile
right now.

_____

_____

_____

_____

_____

_____

_____

_____

Monday, January 8, 2018

In two words, how do you feel right now?

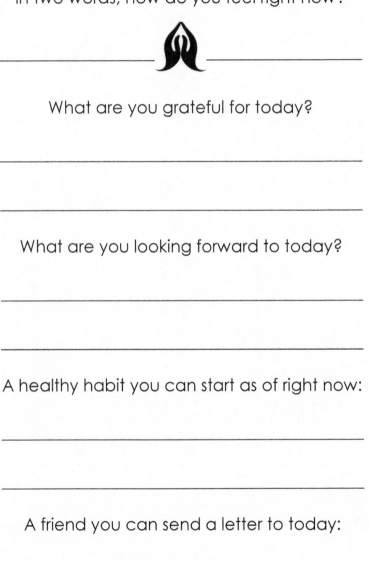

_____ _____

What are you grateful for today?

_____

_____

What are you looking forward to today?

_____

_____

A healthy habit you can start as of right now:

_____

_____

A friend you can send a letter to today:

_____

Tuesday, January 9, 2018

In two words, how do you feel right now?

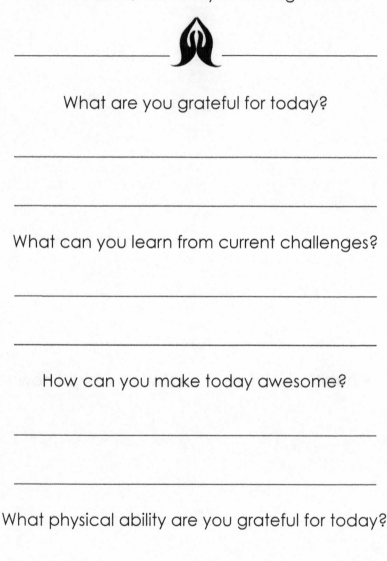

_____   _____

What are you grateful for today?

_____

_____

What can you learn from current challenges?

_____

_____

How can you make today awesome?

_____

_____

What physical ability are you grateful for today?

_____

Wednesday, January 10, 2018

In two words, how do you feel right now?

_____   _____

What are you grateful for today?

_____

_____

What would you like to do more often?

_____

_____

What would you like to do less often?

_____

_____

Modern technology you appreciate today:

_____

Thursday, January 11, 2018

In two words, how do you feel right now?

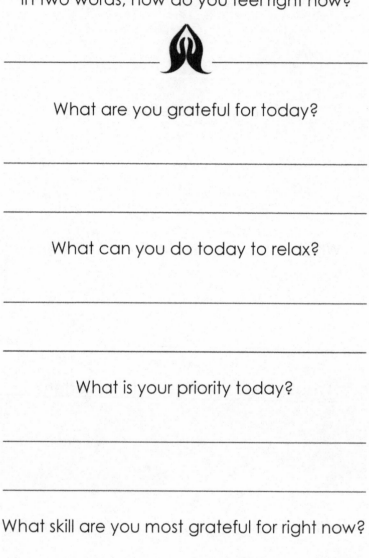

_____   _____

What are you grateful for today?

_____

_____

What can you do today to relax?

_____

_____

What is your priority today?

_____

_____

What skill are you most grateful for right now?

_____

Friday, January 12, 2018

In two words, how do you feel right now?

_____ _____

What are you grateful for today?

_____

_____

What do you have plenty of?

_____

_____

What piece of wisdom are you grateful for?

_____

_____

Which current relationship are you grateful for?

_____

Saturday, January 13, 2018

In two words, how do you feel right now?

_____ ꧁ _____

What are you grateful for today?

_____

_____

What freedoms are you taking for granted?

_____

_____

From where do you gain your sense of self-worth?

_____

_____

What good deed can you do in secret today?

_____

Sunday, January 14, 2018

In two words, how do you feel right now?

_____ _____

What are you grateful for today?

_____

_____

A goal you can accomplish today or get closer to:

_____

_____

What happened this week you want to remember:

_____

_____

How are you exactly the same as everyone else?

_____

Reflections

Note the highlights in your life in this moment.
Write down a quote that motivates you,
the titles of books you want to read
or documentaries to watch,
and a reason to smile
right now.

_____

_____

_____

_____

_____

_____

_____

_____

Monday, January 15, 2018

In two words, how do you feel right now?

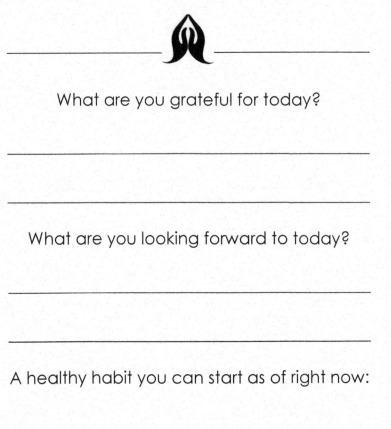

What are you grateful for today?

_____

_____

What are you looking forward to today?

_____

_____

A healthy habit you can start as of right now:

_____

_____

A friend you can send a letter to today:

_____

Tuesday, January 16, 2018

In two words, how do you feel right now?

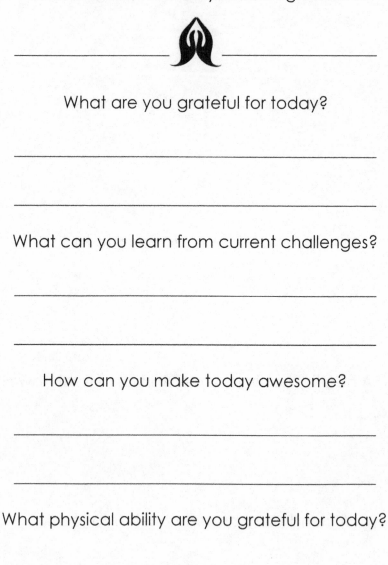

_____   _____

What are you grateful for today?

_____

_____

What can you learn from current challenges?

_____

_____

How can you make today awesome?

_____

_____

What physical ability are you grateful for today?

_____

Wednesday, January 17, 2018

In two words, how do you feel right now?

_____ _____

What are you grateful for today?

_____

_____

What would you like to do more often?

_____

_____

What would you like to do less often?

_____

_____

Modern technology you appreciate today:

_____

Thursday, January 18, 2018

In two words, how do you feel right now?

_____ _____

What are you grateful for today?

_____

_____

What can you do today to relax?

_____

_____

What is your priority today?

_____

_____

What skill are you most grateful for right now?

_____

Friday, January 19, 2018

In two words, how do you feel right now?

_____

What are you grateful for today?

_____

_____

What do you have plenty of?

_____

_____

What piece of wisdom are you grateful for?

_____

_____

Which current relationship are you grateful for?

_____

Saturday, January 20, 2018

In two words, how do you feel right now?

_____   _____

What are you grateful for today?

_____

_____

What freedoms are you taking for granted?

_____

_____

From where do you gain your sense of self-worth?

_____

_____

What good deed can you do in secret today?

_____

Sunday, January 21, 2018

In two words, how do you feel right now?

_____ 🙏 _____

What are you grateful for today?

_____

_____

A goal you can accomplish today or get closer to:

_____

_____

What happened this week you want to remember:

_____

_____

How are you exactly the same as everyone else?

_____

Reflections

Note the highlights in your life in this moment.
Write down a quote that motivates you,
the titles of books you want to read
or documentaries to watch,
and a reason to smile
right now.

_____

_____

_____

_____

_____

_____

_____

_____

Monday, January 22, 2018

In two words, how do you feel right now?

_____

What are you grateful for today?

_____

_____

What are you looking forward to today?

_____

_____

A healthy habit you can start as of right now:

_____

_____

A friend you can send a letter to today:

_____

Tuesday, January 23, 2018

In two words, how do you feel right now?

_____   _____

What are you grateful for today?

_____

_____

What can you learn from current challenges?

_____

_____

How can you make today awesome?

_____

_____

What physical ability are you grateful for today?

_____

Wednesday, January 24, 2018

In two words, how do you feel right now?

_____   _____

What are you grateful for today?

_____

_____

What would you like to do more often?

_____

_____

What would you like to do less often?

_____

_____

Modern technology you appreciate today:

_____

Thursday, January 25, 2018

In two words, how do you feel right now?

_____ _____

What are you grateful for today?

_____

_____

What can you do today to relax?

_____

_____

What is your priority today?

_____

_____

What skill are you most grateful for right now?

_____

Friday, January 26, 2018

In two words, how do you feel right now?

_____ _____

What are you grateful for today?

_____

_____

What do you have plenty of?

_____

_____

What piece of wisdom are you grateful for?

_____

_____

Which current relationship are you grateful for?

_____

Saturday, January 27, 2018

In two words, how do you feel right now?

_____   _____

What are you grateful for today?

_____

_____

What freedoms are you taking for granted?

_____

_____

From where do you gain your sense of self-worth?

_____

_____

What good deed can you do in secret today?

_____

Sunday, January 28, 2018

In two words, how do you feel right now?

_____ _____

What are you grateful for today?

_____

_____

A goal you can accomplish today or get closer to:

_____

_____

What happened this week you want to remember:

_____

_____

How are you exactly the same as everyone else?

_____

Reflections

Note the highlights in your life in this moment.
Write down a quote that motivates you,
the titles of books you want to read
or documentaries to watch,
and a reason to smile
right now.

_____

_____

_____

_____

_____

_____

_____

_____

Monday, January 29, 2018

In two words, how do you feel right now?

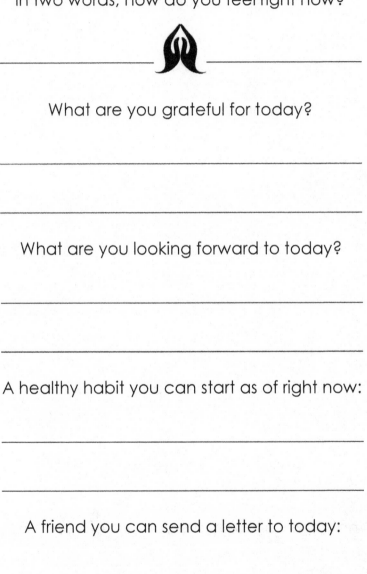

_____   _____

What are you grateful for today?

_____

_____

What are you looking forward to today?

_____

_____

A healthy habit you can start as of right now:

_____

_____

A friend you can send a letter to today:

_____

Tuesday, January 30, 2018

In two words, how do you feel right now?

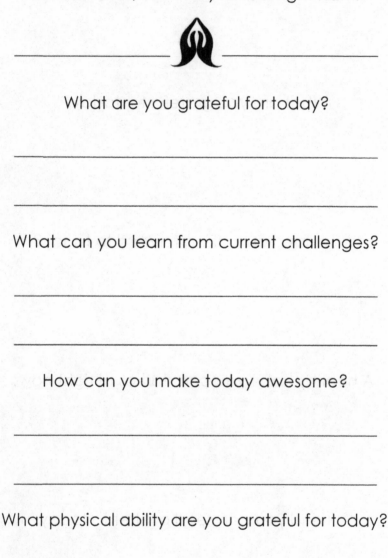

_____   _____

What are you grateful for today?

_____

_____

What can you learn from current challenges?

_____

_____

How can you make today awesome?

_____

_____

What physical ability are you grateful for today?

_____

Wednesday, January 31, 2018

In two words, how do you feel right now?

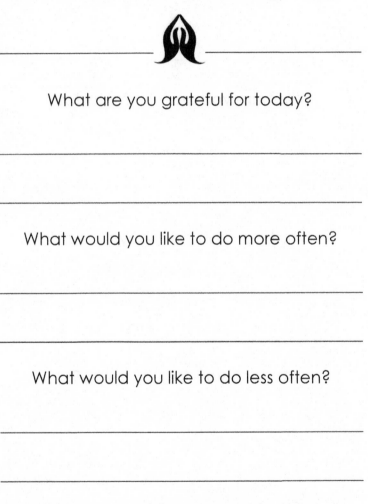

_____ _____

What are you grateful for today?

_____

_____

What would you like to do more often?

_____

_____

What would you like to do less often?

_____

_____

Modern technology you appreciate today:

_____

Thursday, February 1, 2018

In two words, how do you feel right now?

_____

What are you grateful for today?

_____

_____

What can you do today to relax?

_____

_____

What is your priority today?

_____

_____

What skill are you most grateful for right now?

_____

February 1

Friday, February 2, 2018

In two words, how do you feel right now?

_____ _____

What are you grateful for today?

_____

_____

What do you have plenty of?

_____

_____

What piece of wisdom are you grateful for?

_____

_____

Which current relationship are you grateful for?

_____

Saturday, February 3, 2018

In two words, how do you feel right now?

_____   _____

What are you grateful for today?

_____

_____

What freedoms are you taking for granted?

_____

_____

From where do you gain your sense of self-worth?

_____

_____

What good deed can you do in secret today?

_____

Sunday, February 4, 2018

In two words, how do you feel right now?

_____   _____

What are you grateful for today?

_____

_____

A goal you can accomplish today or get closer to:

_____

_____

What happened this week you want to remember:

_____

_____

How are you exactly the same as everyone else?

_____

Reflections

Note the highlights in your life in this moment.
Write down a quote that motivates you,
the titles of books you want to read
or documentaries to watch,
and a reason to smile
right now.

_____

_____

_____

_____

_____

_____

_____

_____

_____

Monday, February 5, 2018

In two words, how do you feel right now?

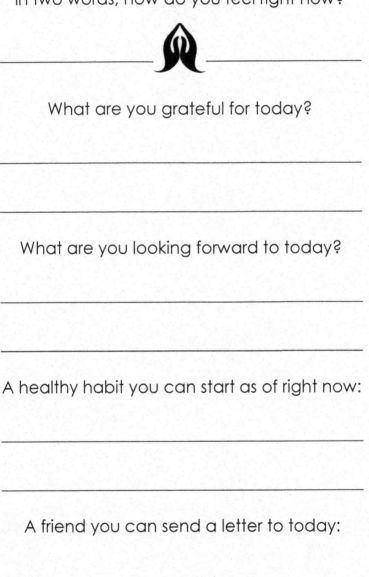

_____   _____

What are you grateful for today?

_____

_____

What are you looking forward to today?

_____

_____

A healthy habit you can start as of right now:

_____

_____

A friend you can send a letter to today:

_____

Tuesday, February 6, 2018

In two words, how do you feel right now?

_____

What are you grateful for today?

_____

_____

What can you learn from current challenges?

_____

_____

How can you make today awesome?

_____

_____

What physical ability are you grateful for today?

_____

Wednesday, February 7, 2018

In two words, how do you feel right now?

_____   _____

What are you grateful for today?

_____

_____

What would you like to do more often?

_____

_____

What would you like to do less often?

_____

_____

Modern technology you appreciate today:

_____

Thursday, February 8, 2018

In two words, how do you feel right now?

_____   _____

What are you grateful for today?

_____

_____

What can you do today to relax?

_____

_____

What is your priority today?

_____

_____

What skill are you most grateful for right now?

_____

Friday, February 9, 2018

In two words, how do you feel right now?

_____ _____

What are you grateful for today?

_____

_____

What do you have plenty of?

_____

_____

What piece of wisdom are you grateful for?

_____

_____

Which current relationship are you grateful for?

_____

Saturday, February 10, 2018

In two words, how do you feel right now?

_____   _____

What are you grateful for today?

_____

_____

What freedoms are you taking for granted?

_____

_____

From where do you gain your sense of self-worth?

_____

_____

What good deed can you do in secret today?

_____

Sunday, February 11, 2018

In two words, how do you feel right now?

_____   _____

What are you grateful for today?

_____

_____

A goal you can accomplish today or get closer to:

_____

_____

What happened this week you want to remember:

_____

_____

How are you exactly the same as everyone else?

_____

Reflections

Note the highlights in your life in this moment.
Write down a quote that motivates you,
the titles of books you want to read
or documentaries to watch,
and a reason to smile
right now.

_____

_____

_____

_____

_____

_____

_____

_____

Monday, February 12, 2018

In two words, how do you feel right now?

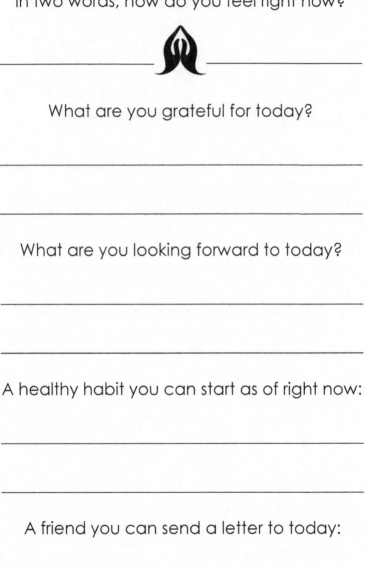

_____   _____

What are you grateful for today?

_____

_____

What are you looking forward to today?

_____

_____

A healthy habit you can start as of right now:

_____

_____

A friend you can send a letter to today:

_____

Tuesday, February 13, 2018

In two words, how do you feel right now?

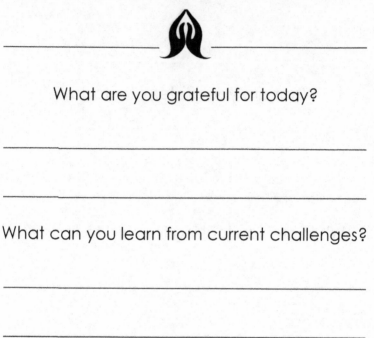

_____   _____

What are you grateful for today?

_____

_____

What can you learn from current challenges?

_____

_____

How can you make today awesome?

_____

_____

What physical ability are you grateful for today?

_____

Wednesday, February 14, 2018

In two words, how do you feel right now?

_____ _____

What are you grateful for today?

_____

_____

What would you like to do more often?

_____

_____

What would you like to do less often?

_____

_____

Modern technology you appreciate today:

_____

Thursday, February 15, 2018

In two words, how do you feel right now?

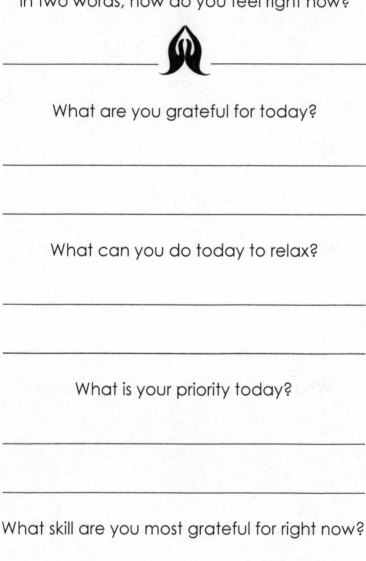

_____

What are you grateful for today?

_____

_____

What can you do today to relax?

_____

_____

What is your priority today?

_____

_____

What skill are you most grateful for right now?

_____

Friday, February 16, 2018

In two words, how do you feel right now?

_____ _____

What are you grateful for today?

_____

_____

What do you have plenty of?

_____

_____

What piece of wisdom are you grateful for?

_____

_____

Which current relationship are you grateful for?

_____

Saturday, February 17, 2018

In two words, how do you feel right now?

_____   _____

What are you grateful for today?

_____

_____

What freedoms are you taking for granted?

_____

_____

From where do you gain your sense of self-worth?

_____

_____

What good deed can you do in secret today?

_____

Sunday, February 18, 2018

In two words, how do you feel right now?

_____ _____

What are you grateful for today?

_____

_____

A goal you can accomplish today or get closer to:

_____

_____

What happened this week you want to remember:

_____

_____

How are you exactly the same as everyone else?

_____

Reflections

Note the highlights in your life in this moment.
Write down a quote that motivates you,
the titles of books you want to read
or documentaries to watch,
and a reason to smile
right now.

_____

_____

_____

_____

_____

_____

_____

_____

Monday, February 19, 2018

In two words, how do you feel right now?

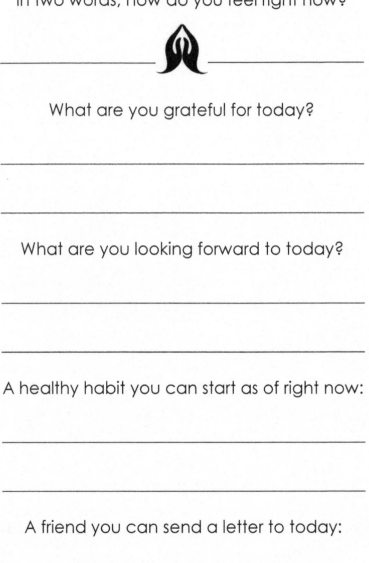

_____   _____

What are you grateful for today?

_____

_____

What are you looking forward to today?

_____

_____

A healthy habit you can start as of right now:

_____

_____

A friend you can send a letter to today:

_____

Tuesday, February 20, 2018

In two words, how do you feel right now?

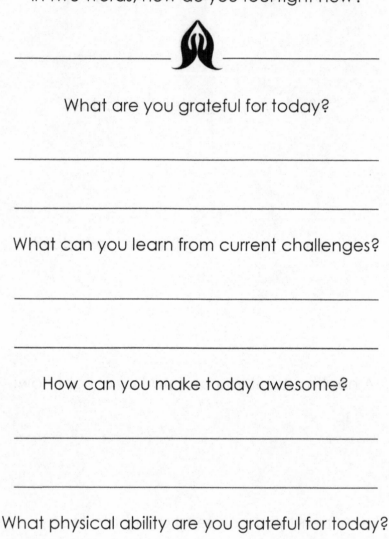

_____ _____

What are you grateful for today?

_____

_____

What can you learn from current challenges?

_____

_____

How can you make today awesome?

_____

_____

What physical ability are you grateful for today?

_____

Wednesday, February 21, 2018

In two words, how do you feel right now?

_____   _____

What are you grateful for today?

_____

_____

What would you like to do more often?

_____

_____

What would you like to do less often?

_____

_____

Modern technology you appreciate today:

_____

Thursday, February 22, 2018

In two words, how do you feel right now?

_____   _____

What are you grateful for today?

_____

_____

What can you do today to relax?

_____

_____

What is your priority today?

_____

_____

What skill are you most grateful for right now?

_____

Friday, February 23, 2018

In two words, how do you feel right now?

_____ _____

What are you grateful for today?

_____

_____

What do you have plenty of?

_____

_____

What piece of wisdom are you grateful for?

_____

_____

Which current relationship are you grateful for?

_____

Saturday, February 24, 2018

In two words, how do you feel right now?

_____ _____

What are you grateful for today?

_____

_____

What freedoms are you taking for granted?

_____

_____

From where do you gain your sense of self-worth?

_____

_____

What good deed can you do in secret today?

_____

Sunday, February 25, 2018

In two words, how do you feel right now?

_____ _____

What are you grateful for today?

_____

_____

A goal you can accomplish today or get closer to:

_____

_____

What happened this week you want to remember:

_____

_____

How are you exactly the same as everyone else?

_____

Reflections

Note the highlights in your life in this moment.
Write down a quote that motivates you,
the titles of books you want to read
or documentaries to watch,
and a reason to smile
right now.

_____

_____

_____

_____

_____

_____

_____

_____

_____

Monday, February 26, 2018

In two words, how do you feel right now?

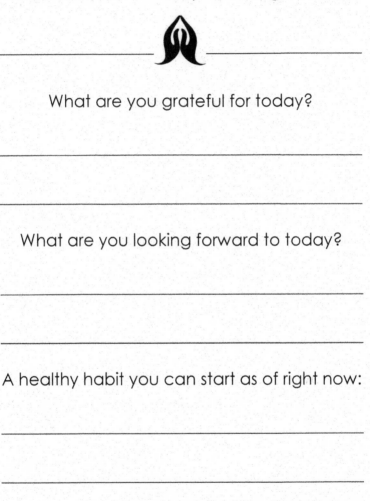

_____   _____

What are you grateful for today?

_____

_____

What are you looking forward to today?

_____

_____

A healthy habit you can start as of right now:

_____

_____

A friend you can send a letter to today:

_____

Tuesday, February 27, 2018

In two words, how do you feel right now?

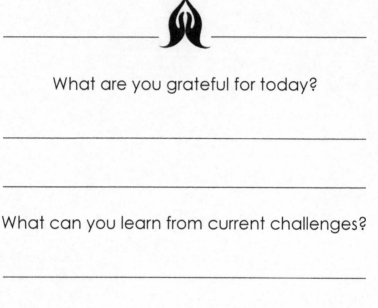

_____ _____

What are you grateful for today?

_____

_____

What can you learn from current challenges?

_____

_____

How can you make today awesome?

_____

_____

What physical ability are you grateful for today?

_____

February 27

Wednesday, February 28, 2018

In two words, how do you feel right now?

_____   _____

What are you grateful for today?

_____

_____

What would you like to do more often?

_____

_____

What would you like to do less often?

_____

_____

Modern technology you appreciate today:

_____

Thursday, March 1, 2018

In two words, how do you feel right now?

_____ _____

What are you grateful for today?

_____

_____

What can you do today to relax?

_____

_____

What is your priority today?

_____

_____

What skill are you most grateful for right now?

_____

Friday, March 2, 2018

In two words, how do you feel right now?

_____ — _____

What are you grateful for today?

_____

_____

What do you have plenty of?

_____

_____

What piece of wisdom are you grateful for?

_____

_____

Which current relationship are you grateful for?

_____

Saturday, March 3, 2018

In two words, how do you feel right now?

_____   _____

What are you grateful for today?

_____

_____

What freedoms are you taking for granted?

_____

_____

From where do you gain your sense of self-worth?

_____

_____

What good deed can you do in secret today?

_____

Sunday, March 4, 2018

In two words, how do you feel right now?

_____ _____

What are you grateful for today?

_____

_____

A goal you can accomplish today or get closer to:

_____

_____

What happened this week you want to remember:

_____

_____

How are you exactly the same as everyone else?

_____

Reflections

Note the highlights in your life in this moment.
Write down a quote that motivates you,
the titles of books you want to read
or documentaries to watch,
and a reason to smile
right now.

_____

_____

_____

_____

_____

_____

_____

_____

Monday, March 5, 2018

In two words, how do you feel right now?

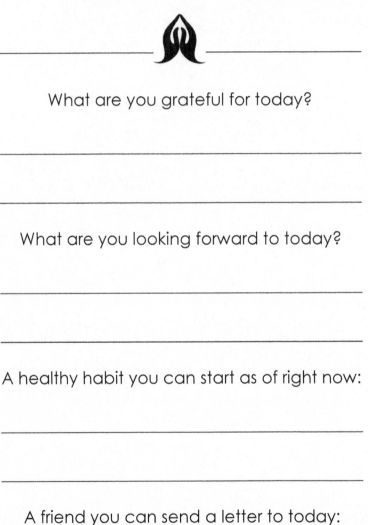

_____ _____

What are you grateful for today?

_____

_____

What are you looking forward to today?

_____

_____

A healthy habit you can start as of right now:

_____

_____

A friend you can send a letter to today:

_____

Tuesday, March 6, 2018

In two words, how do you feel right now?

_____   _____

What are you grateful for today?

_____

_____

What can you learn from current challenges?

_____

_____

How can you make today awesome?

_____

_____

What physical ability are you grateful for today?

_____

Wednesday, March 7, 2018

In two words, how do you feel right now?

_____   _____

What are you grateful for today?

_____

_____

What would you like to do more often?

_____

_____

What would you like to do less often?

_____

_____

Modern technology you appreciate today:

_____

Thursday, March 8, 2018

In two words, how do you feel right now?

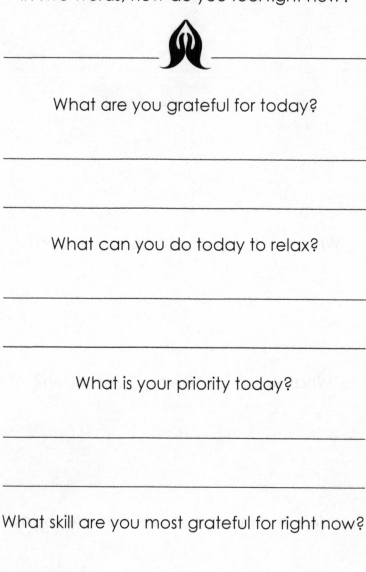

_____   _____

What are you grateful for today?

_____

_____

What can you do today to relax?

_____

_____

What is your priority today?

_____

_____

What skill are you most grateful for right now?

_____

Friday, March 9, 2018

In two words, how do you feel right now?

_____ _____

What are you grateful for today?

_____

_____

What do you have plenty of?

_____

_____

What piece of wisdom are you grateful for?

_____

_____

Which current relationship are you grateful for?

_____

Saturday, March 10, 2018

In two words, how do you feel right now?

_____ _____

What are you grateful for today?

_____

_____

What freedoms are you taking for granted?

_____

_____

From where do you gain your sense of self-worth?

_____

_____

What good deed can you do in secret today?

_____

Sunday, March 11, 2018

In two words, how do you feel right now?

_____ _____

What are you grateful for today?

_____

_____

A goal you can accomplish today or get closer to:

_____

_____

What happened this week you want to remember:

_____

_____

How are you exactly the same as everyone else?

_____

Reflections

Note the highlights in your life in this moment.
Write down a quote that motivates you,
the titles of books you want to read
or documentaries to watch,
and a reason to smile
right now.

_____

_____

_____

_____

_____

_____

_____

_____

_____

Monday, March 12, 2018

In two words, how do you feel right now?

_____   _____

What are you grateful for today?

_____

_____

What are you looking forward to today?

_____

_____

A healthy habit you can start as of right now:

_____

_____

A friend you can send a letter to today:

_____

Tuesday, March 13, 2018

In two words, how do you feel right now?

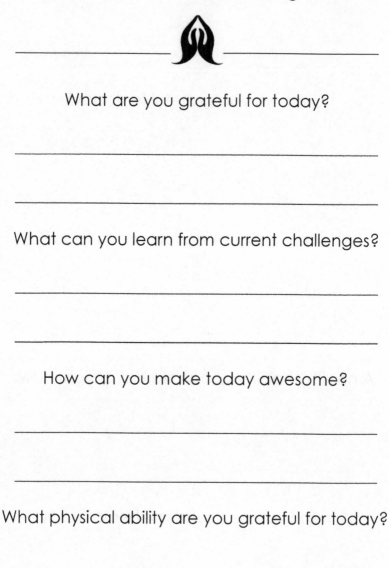

_____ _____

What are you grateful for today?

_____

_____

What can you learn from current challenges?

_____

_____

How can you make today awesome?

_____

_____

What physical ability are you grateful for today?

_____

Wednesday, March 14, 2018

In two words, how do you feel right now?

_____   _____

What are you grateful for today?

_____

_____

What would you like to do more often?

_____

_____

What would you like to do less often?

_____

_____

Modern technology you appreciate today:

_____

Thursday, March 15, 2018

In two words, how do you feel right now?

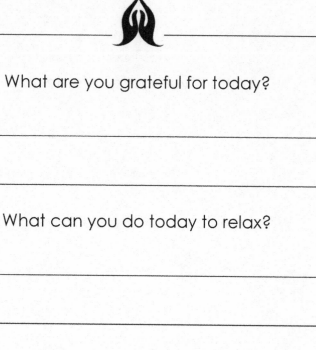

_____   _____

What are you grateful for today?

_____

_____

What can you do today to relax?

_____

_____

What is your priority today?

_____

_____

What skill are you most grateful for right now?

_____

Friday, March 16, 2018

In two words, how do you feel right now?

_____   🙏   _____

What are you grateful for today?

_____

_____

What do you have plenty of?

_____

_____

What piece of wisdom are you grateful for?

_____

_____

Which current relationship are you grateful for?

_____

Saturday, March 17, 2018

In two words, how do you feel right now?

_____   _____

What are you grateful for today?

_____

_____

What freedoms are you taking for granted?

_____

_____

From where do you gain your sense of self-worth?

_____

_____

What good deed can you do in secret today?

_____

Sunday, March 18, 2018

In two words, how do you feel right now?

_____ _____

What are you grateful for today?

_____

_____

A goal you can accomplish today or get closer to:

_____

_____

What happened this week you want to remember:

_____

_____

How are you exactly the same as everyone else?

_____

Reflections

Note the highlights in your life in this moment.
Write down a quote that motivates you,
the titles of books you want to read
or documentaries to watch,
and a reason to smile
right now.

_____

_____

_____

_____

_____

_____

_____

_____

_____

Monday, March 19, 2018

In two words, how do you feel right now?

_____ _____

What are you grateful for today?

_____

_____

What are you looking forward to today?

_____

_____

A healthy habit you can start as of right now:

_____

_____

A friend you can send a letter to today:

_____

Tuesday, March 20, 2018

In two words, how do you feel right now?

_____   _____

What are you grateful for today?

_____

_____

What can you learn from current challenges?

_____

_____

How can you make today awesome?

_____

_____

What physical ability are you grateful for today?

_____

Wednesday, March 21, 2018

In two words, how do you feel right now?

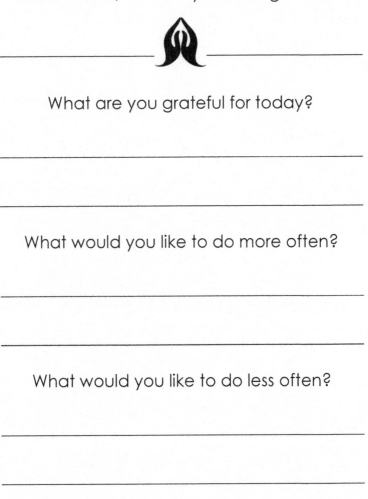

_____   _____

What are you grateful for today?

_____

_____

What would you like to do more often?

_____

_____

What would you like to do less often?

_____

_____

Modern technology you appreciate today:

_____

Thursday, March 22, 2018

In two words, how do you feel right now?

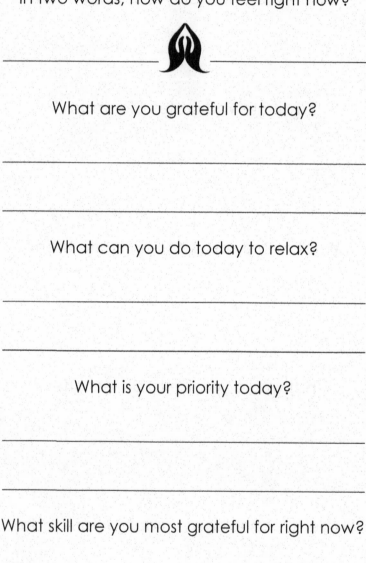

_____   _____

What are you grateful for today?

_____

_____

What can you do today to relax?

_____

_____

What is your priority today?

_____

_____

What skill are you most grateful for right now?

_____

Friday, March 23, 2018

In two words, how do you feel right now?

_____   _____

What are you grateful for today?

_____

_____

What do you have plenty of?

_____

_____

What piece of wisdom are you grateful for?

_____

_____

Which current relationship are you grateful for?

_____

Saturday, March 24, 2018

In two words, how do you feel right now?

_____ _____

What are you grateful for today?

_____

_____

What freedoms are you taking for granted?

_____

_____

From where do you gain your sense of self-worth?

_____

_____

What good deed can you do in secret today?

_____

Sunday, March 25, 2018

In two words, how do you feel right now?

_____ _____

What are you grateful for today?

_____

_____

A goal you can accomplish today or get closer to:

_____

_____

What happened this week you want to remember:

_____

_____

How are you exactly the same as everyone else?

_____

Reflections

Note the highlights in your life in this moment.
Write down a quote that motivates you,
the titles of books you want to read
or documentaries to watch,
and a reason to smile
right now.

_____

_____

_____

_____

_____

_____

_____

_____

_____

Monday, March 26, 2018

In two words, how do you feel right now?

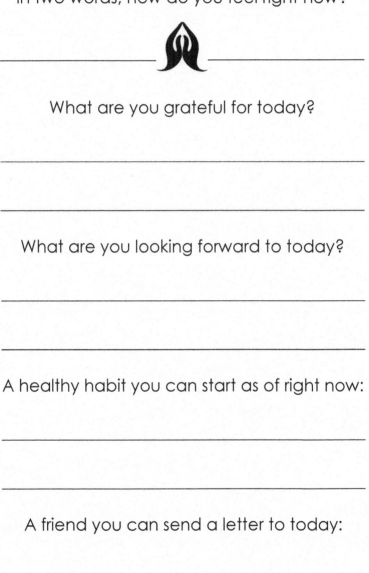

_____   _____

What are you grateful for today?

_____

_____

What are you looking forward to today?

_____

_____

A healthy habit you can start as of right now:

_____

_____

A friend you can send a letter to today:

_____

Tuesday, March 27, 2018

In two words, how do you feel right now?

_____ _____

What are you grateful for today?

_____

_____

What can you learn from current challenges?

_____

_____

How can you make today awesome?

_____

_____

What physical ability are you grateful for today?

_____

Wednesday, March 28, 2018

In two words, how do you feel right now?

_____ _____

What are you grateful for today?

_____

_____

What would you like to do more often?

_____

_____

What would you like to do less often?

_____

_____

Modern technology you appreciate today:

_____

Thursday, March 29, 2018

In two words, how do you feel right now?

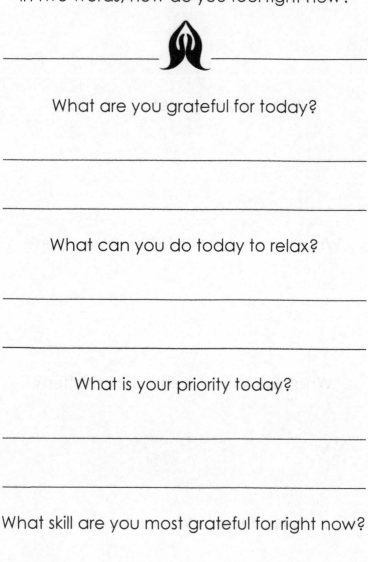

_____   _____

What are you grateful for today?

_____

_____

What can you do today to relax?

_____

_____

What is your priority today?

_____

_____

What skill are you most grateful for right now?

_____

Friday, March 30, 2018

In two words, how do you feel right now?

_____   _____

What are you grateful for today?

_____

_____

What do you have plenty of?

_____

_____

What piece of wisdom are you grateful for?

_____

_____

Which current relationship are you grateful for?

_____

Saturday, March 31, 2018

In two words, how do you feel right now?

_____   _____

What are you grateful for today?

_____

_____

What freedoms are you taking for granted?

_____

_____

From where do you gain your sense of self-worth?

_____

_____

What good deed can you do in secret today?

_____

Sunday, April 1, 2018

In two words, how do you feel right now?

_____ _____

What are you grateful for today?

_____

_____

A goal you can accomplish today or get closer to:

_____

_____

What happened this week you want to remember:

_____

_____

How are you exactly the same as everyone else?

_____

Reflections

Note the highlights in your life in this moment.
Write down a quote that motivates you,
the titles of books you want to read
or documentaries to watch,
and a reason to smile
right now.

_____

_____

_____

_____

_____

_____

_____

_____

Monday, April 2, 2018

In two words, how do you feel right now?

_____   _____

What are you grateful for today?

_____

_____

What are you looking forward to today?

_____

_____

A healthy habit you can start as of right now:

_____

_____

A friend you can send a letter to today:

_____

Tuesday, April 3, 2018

In two words, how do you feel right now?

_____ _____

What are you grateful for today?

_____

_____

What can you learn from current challenges?

_____

_____

How can you make today awesome?

_____

_____

What physical ability are you grateful for today?

_____

Wednesday, April 4, 2018

In two words, how do you feel right now?

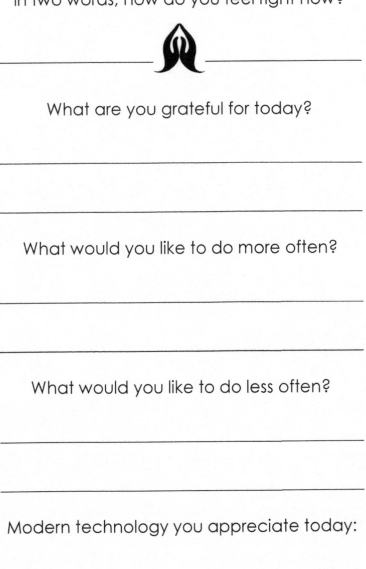

_____   _____

What are you grateful for today?

_____

_____

What would you like to do more often?

_____

_____

What would you like to do less often?

_____

_____

Modern technology you appreciate today:

_____

Thursday, April 5, 2018

In two words, how do you feel right now?

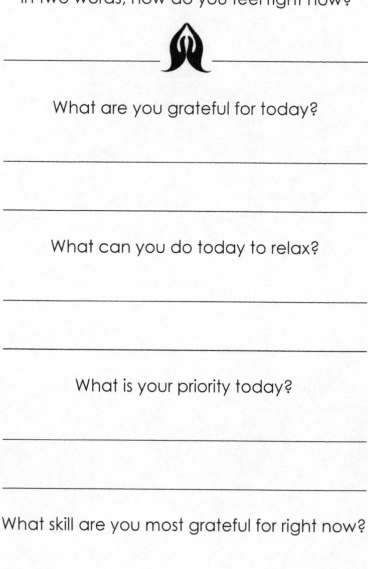

_____   _____

What are you grateful for today?

_____

_____

What can you do today to relax?

_____

_____

What is your priority today?

_____

_____

What skill are you most grateful for right now?

_____

Friday, April 6, 2018

In two words, how do you feel right now?

_____   _____

What are you grateful for today?

_____

_____

What do you have plenty of?

_____

_____

What piece of wisdom are you grateful for?

_____

_____

Which current relationship are you grateful for?

_____

Saturday, April 7, 2018

In two words, how do you feel right now?

_____ _____

What are you grateful for today?

_____

_____

What freedoms are you taking for granted?

_____

_____

From where do you gain your sense of self-worth?

_____

_____

What good deed can you do in secret today?

_____

Sunday, April 8, 2018

In two words, how do you feel right now?

_____ 🙏 _____

What are you grateful for today?

_____

_____

A goal you can accomplish today or get closer to:

_____

_____

What happened this week you want to remember:

_____

_____

How are you exactly the same as everyone else?

_____

Reflections

Note the highlights in your life in this moment.
Write down a quote that motivates you,
the titles of books you want to read
or documentaries to watch,
and a reason to smile
right now.

_____

_____

_____

_____

_____

_____

_____

_____

Monday, April 9, 2018

In two words, how do you feel right now?

_____ _____

What are you grateful for today?

_____

_____

What are you looking forward to today?

_____

_____

A healthy habit you can start as of right now:

_____

_____

A friend you can send a letter to today:

_____

Tuesday, April 10, 2018

In two words, how do you feel right now?

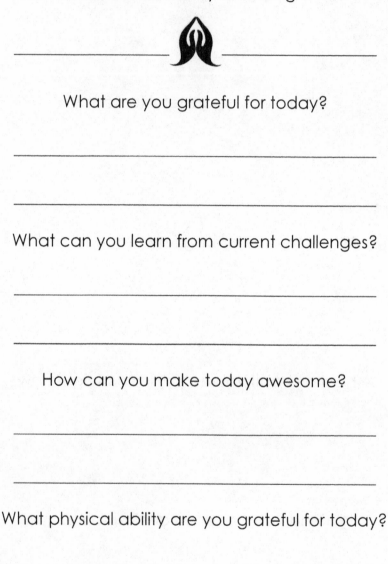

_____   _____

What are you grateful for today?

_____

_____

What can you learn from current challenges?

_____

_____

How can you make today awesome?

_____

_____

What physical ability are you grateful for today?

_____

Wednesday, April 11, 2018

In two words, how do you feel right now?

_____   _____

What are you grateful for today?

_____

_____

What would you like to do more often?

_____

_____

What would you like to do less often?

_____

_____

Modern technology you appreciate today:

_____

Thursday, April 12, 2018

In two words, how do you feel right now?

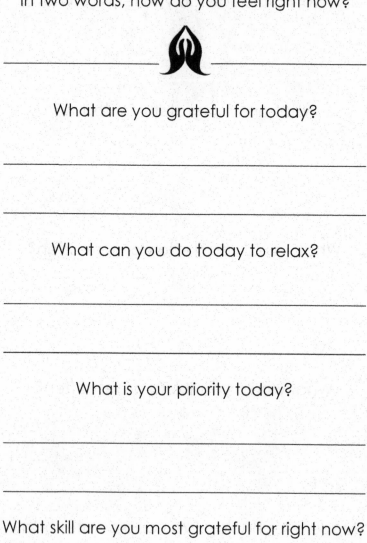

_____   _____

What are you grateful for today?

_____

_____

What can you do today to relax?

_____

_____

What is your priority today?

_____

_____

What skill are you most grateful for right now?

_____

Friday, April 13, 2018

In two words, how do you feel right now?

_____   _____

What are you grateful for today?

_____

_____

What do you have plenty of?

_____

_____

What piece of wisdom are you grateful for?

_____

_____

Which current relationship are you grateful for?

_____

Saturday, April 14, 2018

In two words, how do you feel right now?

_____ 🙏 _____

What are you grateful for today?

_____

_____

What freedoms are you taking for granted?

_____

_____

From where do you gain your sense of self-worth?

_____

_____

What good deed can you do in secret today?

_____

Sunday, April 15, 2018

In two words, how do you feel right now?

_____ _____

What are you grateful for today?

_____

_____

A goal you can accomplish today or get closer to:

_____

_____

What happened this week you want to remember:

_____

_____

How are you exactly the same as everyone else?

_____

Reflections

Note the highlights in your life in this moment.
Write down a quote that motivates you,
the titles of books you want to read
or documentaries to watch,
and a reason to smile
right now.

_____

_____

_____

_____

_____

_____

_____

_____

Monday, April 16, 2018

In two words, how do you feel right now?

_____ _____

What are you grateful for today?

_____

_____

What are you looking forward to today?

_____

_____

A healthy habit you can start as of right now:

_____

_____

A friend you can send a letter to today:

_____

Tuesday, April 17, 2018

In two words, how do you feel right now?

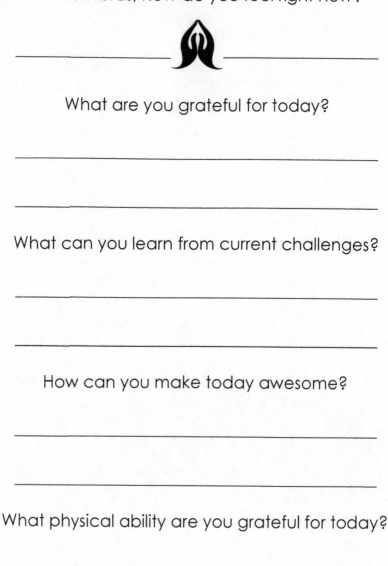

_____ _____

What are you grateful for today?

_____

_____

What can you learn from current challenges?

_____

_____

How can you make today awesome?

_____

_____

What physical ability are you grateful for today?

_____

Wednesday, April 18, 2018

In two words, how do you feel right now?

_____ _____

What are you grateful for today?

_____

_____

What would you like to do more often?

_____

_____

What would you like to do less often?

_____

_____

Modern technology you appreciate today:

_____

Thursday, April 19, 2018

In two words, how do you feel right now?

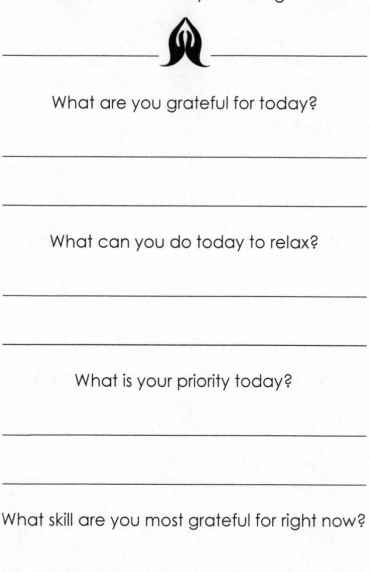

_____   _____

What are you grateful for today?

_____

_____

What can you do today to relax?

_____

_____

What is your priority today?

_____

_____

What skill are you most grateful for right now?

_____

Friday, April 20, 2018

In two words, how do you feel right now?

_____ _____

What are you grateful for today?

_____

_____

What do you have plenty of?

_____

_____

What piece of wisdom are you grateful for?

_____

_____

Which current relationship are you grateful for?

_____

Saturday, April 21, 2018

In two words, how do you feel right now?

_____   _____

What are you grateful for today?

_____

_____

What freedoms are you taking for granted?

_____

_____

From where do you gain your sense of self-worth?

_____

_____

What good deed can you do in secret today?

_____

Sunday, April 22, 2018

In two words, how do you feel right now?

_____ _____

What are you grateful for today?

_____

_____

A goal you can accomplish today or get closer to:

_____

_____

What happened this week you want to remember:

_____

_____

How are you exactly the same as everyone else?

_____

Reflections

Note the highlights in your life in this moment.
Write down a quote that motivates you,
the titles of books you want to read
or documentaries to watch,
and a reason to smile
right now.

_____

_____

_____

_____

_____

_____

_____

_____

Monday, April 23, 2018

In two words, how do you feel right now?

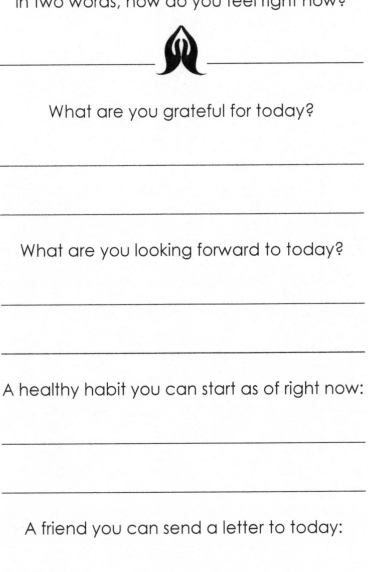

_____   _____

What are you grateful for today?

_____

_____

What are you looking forward to today?

_____

_____

A healthy habit you can start as of right now:

_____

_____

A friend you can send a letter to today:

_____

Tuesday, April 24, 2018

In two words, how do you feel right now?

_____   _____

What are you grateful for today?

_____

_____

What can you learn from current challenges?

_____

_____

How can you make today awesome?

_____

_____

What physical ability are you grateful for today?

_____

Wednesday, April 25, 2018

In two words, how do you feel right now?

_____   _____

What are you grateful for today?

_____

_____

What would you like to do more often?

_____

_____

What would you like to do less often?

_____

_____

Modern technology you appreciate today:

_____

Thursday, April 26, 2018

In two words, how do you feel right now?

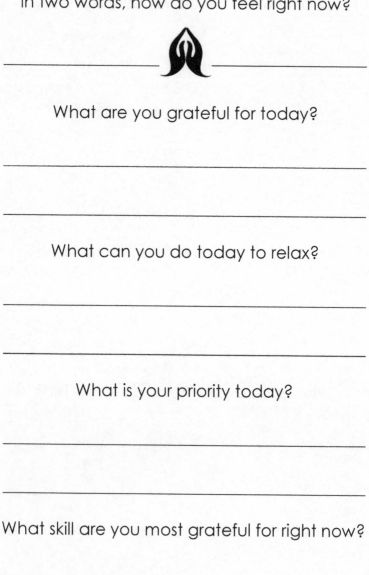

_____   _____

What are you grateful for today?

_____

_____

What can you do today to relax?

_____

_____

What is your priority today?

_____

_____

What skill are you most grateful for right now?

_____

Friday, April 27, 2018

In two words, how do you feel right now?

_____   _____

What are you grateful for today?

_____

_____

What do you have plenty of?

_____

_____

What piece of wisdom are you grateful for?

_____

_____

Which current relationship are you grateful for?

_____

Saturday, April 28, 2018

In two words, how do you feel right now?

_____   _____

What are you grateful for today?

_____

_____

What freedoms are you taking for granted?

_____

_____

From where do you gain your sense of self-worth?

_____

_____

What good deed can you do in secret today?

_____

April 28

Sunday, April 29, 2018

In two words, how do you feel right now?

_____   _____

What are you grateful for today?

_____

_____

A goal you can accomplish today or get closer to:

_____

_____

What happened this week you want to remember:

_____

_____

How are you exactly the same as everyone else?

_____

Reflections

Note the highlights in your life in this moment.
Write down a quote that motivates you,
the titles of books you want to read
or documentaries to watch,
and a reason to smile
right now.

_____

_____

_____

_____

_____

_____

_____

_____

Monday, April 30, 2018

In two words, how do you feel right now?

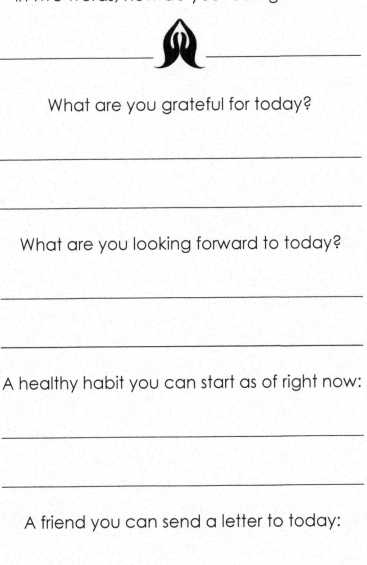

_____   _____

What are you grateful for today?

_____

_____

What are you looking forward to today?

_____

_____

A healthy habit you can start as of right now:

_____

_____

A friend you can send a letter to today:

_____

Tuesday, May 1, 2018

In two words, how do you feel right now?

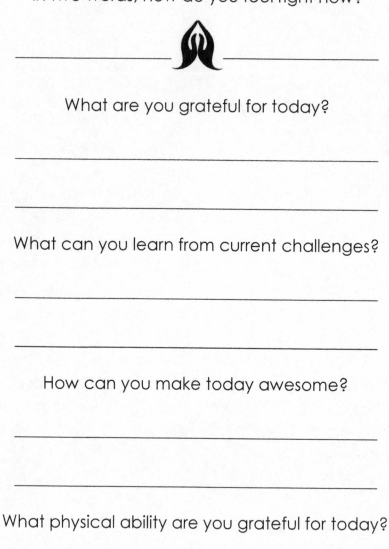

_____   _____

What are you grateful for today?

_____

_____

What can you learn from current challenges?

_____

_____

How can you make today awesome?

_____

_____

What physical ability are you grateful for today?

_____

Wednesday, May 2, 2018

In two words, how do you feel right now?

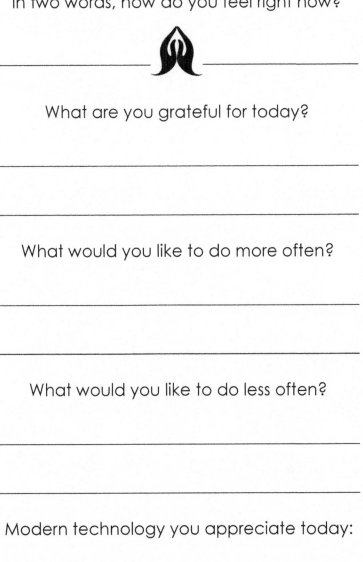

_____   _____

What are you grateful for today?

_____

_____

What would you like to do more often?

_____

_____

What would you like to do less often?

_____

_____

Modern technology you appreciate today:

_____

Thursday, May 3, 2018

In two words, how do you feel right now?

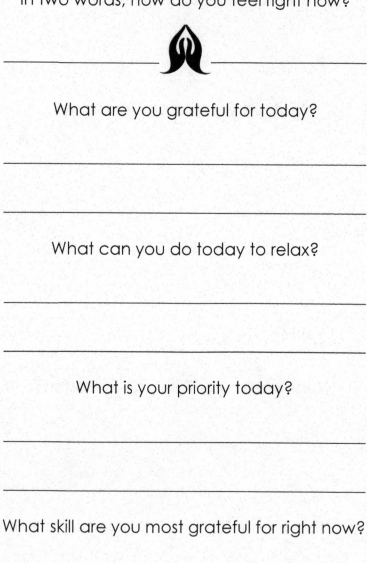

_____   _____

What are you grateful for today?

_____

_____

What can you do today to relax?

_____

_____

What is your priority today?

_____

_____

What skill are you most grateful for right now?

_____

Friday, May 4, 2018

In two words, how do you feel right now?

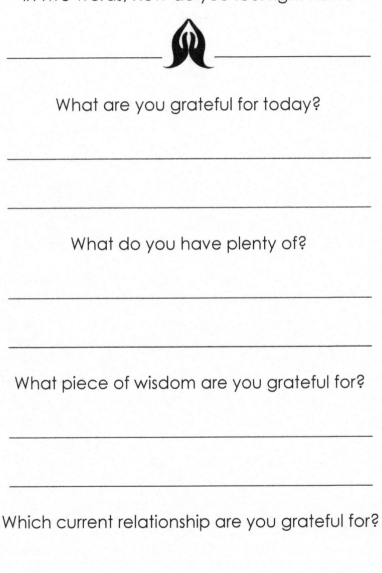

_____   _____

What are you grateful for today?

_____

_____

What do you have plenty of?

_____

_____

What piece of wisdom are you grateful for?

_____

_____

Which current relationship are you grateful for?

_____

Saturday, May 5, 2018

In two words, how do you feel right now?

_____   _____

What are you grateful for today?

_____

_____

What freedoms are you taking for granted?

_____

_____

From where do you gain your sense of self-worth?

_____

_____

What good deed can you do in secret today?

_____

Sunday, May 6, 2018

In two words, how do you feel right now?

_____   _____

What are you grateful for today?

_____

_____

A goal you can accomplish today or get closer to:

_____

_____

What happened this week you want to remember:

_____

_____

How are you exactly the same as everyone else?

_____

Reflections

Note the highlights in your life in this moment.
Write down a quote that motivates you,
the titles of books you want to read
or documentaries to watch,
and a reason to smile
right now.

_____

_____

_____

_____

_____

_____

_____

_____

_____

Monday, May 7, 2018

In two words, how do you feel right now?

_____   _____

What are you grateful for today?

_____

_____

What are you looking forward to today?

_____

_____

A healthy habit you can start as of right now:

_____

_____

A friend you can send a letter to today:

_____

Tuesday, May 8, 2018

In two words, how do you feel right now?

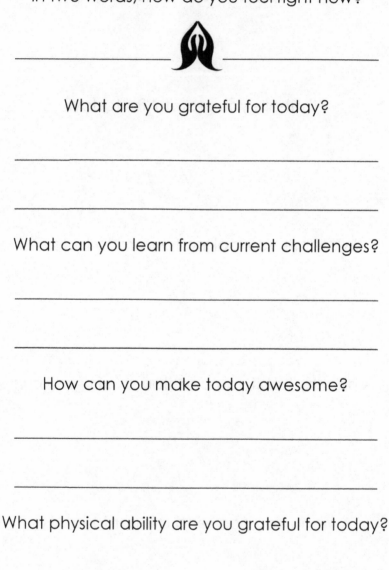

_____   _____

What are you grateful for today?

_____

_____

What can you learn from current challenges?

_____

_____

How can you make today awesome?

_____

_____

What physical ability are you grateful for today?

_____

Wednesday, May 9, 2018

In two words, how do you feel right now?

_____   _____

What are you grateful for today?

_____

_____

What would you like to do more often?

_____

_____

What would you like to do less often?

_____

_____

Modern technology you appreciate today:

_____

Thursday, May 10, 2018

In two words, how do you feel right now?

_____ _____

What are you grateful for today?

_____

_____

What can you do today to relax?

_____

_____

What is your priority today?

_____

_____

What skill are you most grateful for right now?

_____

Friday, May 11, 2018

In two words, how do you feel right now?

_____   _____

What are you grateful for today?

_____

_____

What do you have plenty of?

_____

_____

What piece of wisdom are you grateful for?

_____

_____

Which current relationship are you grateful for?

_____

Saturday, May 12, 2018

In two words, how do you feel right now?

_____   _____

What are you grateful for today?

_____

_____

What freedoms are you taking for granted?

_____

_____

From where do you gain your sense of self-worth?

_____

_____

What good deed can you do in secret today?

_____

Sunday, May 13, 2018

In two words, how do you feel right now?

_____   _____

What are you grateful for today?

_____

_____

A goal you can accomplish today or get closer to:

_____

_____

What happened this week you want to remember:

_____

_____

How are you exactly the same as everyone else?

_____

Reflections

Note the highlights in your life in this moment.
Write down a quote that motivates you,
the titles of books you want to read
or documentaries to watch,
and a reason to smile
right now.

_____

_____

_____

_____

_____

_____

_____

_____

Monday, May 14, 2018

In two words, how do you feel right now?

_____   _____

What are you grateful for today?

_____

_____

What are you looking forward to today?

_____

_____

A healthy habit you can start as of right now:

_____

_____

A friend you can send a letter to today:

_____

Tuesday, May 15, 2018

In two words, how do you feel right now?

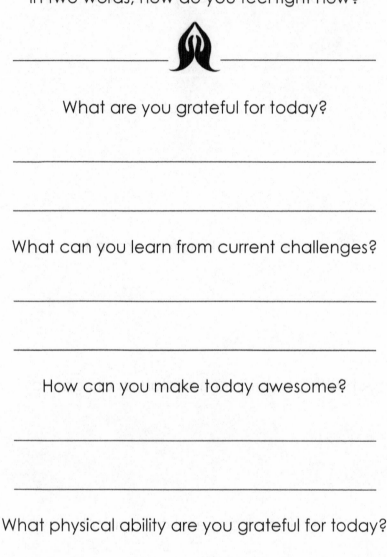

_____   _____

What are you grateful for today?

_____

_____

What can you learn from current challenges?

_____

_____

How can you make today awesome?

_____

_____

What physical ability are you grateful for today?

_____

Wednesday, May 16, 2018

In two words, how do you feel right now?

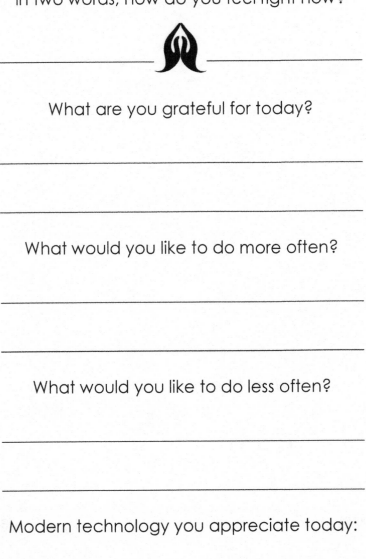

_____   _____

What are you grateful for today?

_____

_____

What would you like to do more often?

_____

_____

What would you like to do less often?

_____

_____

Modern technology you appreciate today:

_____

Thursday, May 17, 2018

In two words, how do you feel right now?

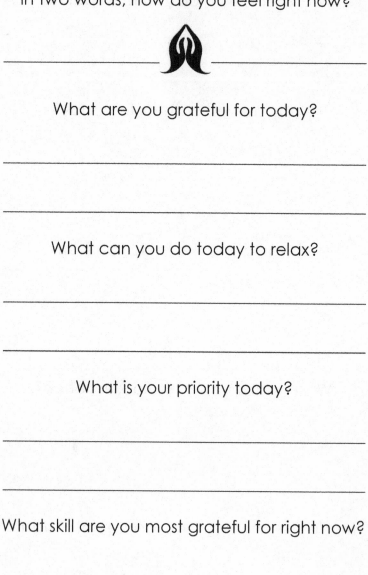

_____   _____

What are you grateful for today?

_____

_____

What can you do today to relax?

_____

_____

What is your priority today?

_____

_____

What skill are you most grateful for right now?

_____

Friday, May 18, 2018

In two words, how do you feel right now?

_____   _____

What are you grateful for today?

_____

_____

What do you have plenty of?

_____

_____

What piece of wisdom are you grateful for?

_____

_____

Which current relationship are you grateful for?

_____

Saturday, May 19, 2018

In two words, how do you feel right now?

_____   _____

What are you grateful for today?

_____

_____

What freedoms are you taking for granted?

_____

_____

From where do you gain your sense of self-worth?

_____

_____

What good deed can you do in secret today?

_____

Sunday, May 20, 2018

In two words, how do you feel right now?

_____ _____

What are you grateful for today?

_____

_____

A goal you can accomplish today or get closer to:

_____

_____

What happened this week you want to remember:

_____

_____

How are you exactly the same as everyone else?

_____

Reflections

Note the highlights in your life in this moment.
Write down a quote that motivates you,
the titles of books you want to read
or documentaries to watch,
and a reason to smile
right now.

_____

_____

_____

_____

_____

_____

_____

_____

_____

Monday, May 21, 2018

In two words, how do you feel right now?

_____   _____

What are you grateful for today?

_____

_____

What are you looking forward to today?

_____

_____

A healthy habit you can start as of right now:

_____

_____

A friend you can send a letter to today:

_____

Tuesday, May 22, 2018

In two words, how do you feel right now?

_____ _____

What are you grateful for today?

_____

_____

What can you learn from current challenges?

_____

_____

How can you make today awesome?

_____

_____

What physical ability are you grateful for today?

_____

Wednesday, May 23, 2018

In two words, how do you feel right now?

_____   _____

What are you grateful for today?

_____

_____

What would you like to do more often?

_____

_____

What would you like to do less often?

_____

_____

Modern technology you appreciate today:

_____

Thursday, May 24, 2018

In two words, how do you feel right now?

_____   _____

What are you grateful for today?

_____

_____

What can you do today to relax?

_____

_____

What is your priority today?

_____

_____

What skill are you most grateful for right now?

_____

Friday, May 25, 2018

In two words, how do you feel right now?

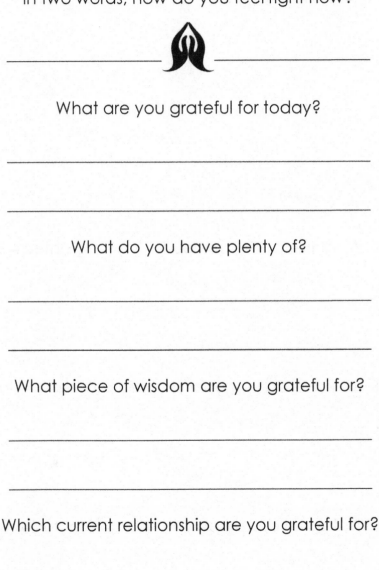

_____   _____

What are you grateful for today?

_____

_____

What do you have plenty of?

_____

_____

What piece of wisdom are you grateful for?

_____

_____

Which current relationship are you grateful for?

_____

Saturday, May 26, 2018

In two words, how do you feel right now?

_____ _____

What are you grateful for today?

_____

_____

What freedoms are you taking for granted?

_____

_____

From where do you gain your sense of self-worth?

_____

_____

What good deed can you do in secret today?

_____

Sunday, May 27, 2018

In two words, how do you feel right now?

_____ _____

What are you grateful for today?

_____

_____

A goal you can accomplish today or get closer to:

_____

_____

What happened this week you want to remember:

_____

_____

How are you exactly the same as everyone else?

_____

Reflections

Note the highlights in your life in this moment.
Write down a quote that motivates you,
the titles of books you want to read
or documentaries to watch,
and a reason to smile
right now.

_____

_____

_____

_____

_____

_____

_____

_____

_____

Monday, May 28, 2018

In two words, how do you feel right now?

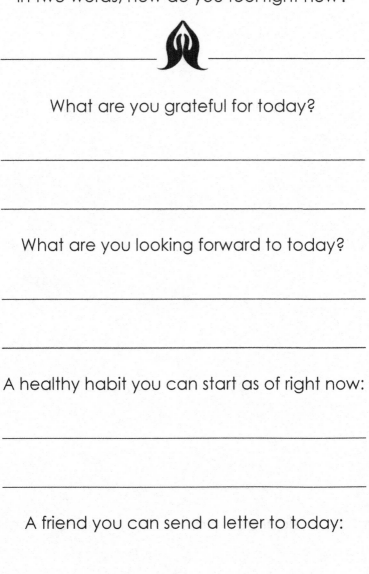

_____   _____

What are you grateful for today?

_____

_____

What are you looking forward to today?

_____

_____

A healthy habit you can start as of right now:

_____

_____

A friend you can send a letter to today:

_____

Tuesday, May 29, 2018

In two words, how do you feel right now?

_____   _____

What are you grateful for today?

_____

_____

What can you learn from current challenges?

_____

_____

How can you make today awesome?

_____

_____

What physical ability are you grateful for today?

_____

Wednesday, May 30, 2018

In two words, how do you feel right now?

_____   _____

What are you grateful for today?

_____

_____

What would you like to do more often?

_____

_____

What would you like to do less often?

_____

_____

Modern technology you appreciate today:

_____

Thursday, May 31, 2018

In two words, how do you feel right now?

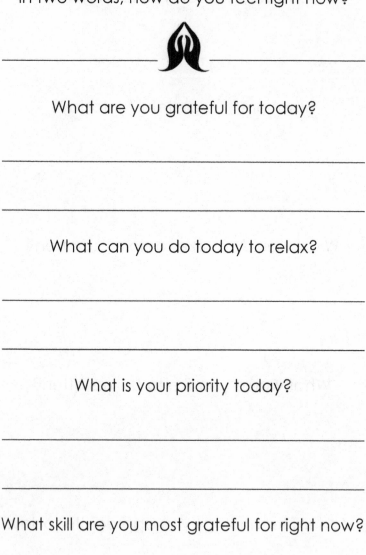

_____   _____

What are you grateful for today?

_____

_____

What can you do today to relax?

_____

_____

What is your priority today?

_____

_____

What skill are you most grateful for right now?

_____

Friday, June 1, 2018

In two words, how do you feel right now?

_____   _____

What are you grateful for today?

_____

_____

What do you have plenty of?

_____

_____

What piece of wisdom are you grateful for?

_____

_____

Which current relationship are you grateful for?

_____

Saturday, June 2, 2018

In two words, how do you feel right now?

_____   _____

What are you grateful for today?

_____

_____

What freedoms are you taking for granted?

_____

_____

From where do you gain your sense of self-worth?

_____

_____

What good deed can you do in secret today?

_____

Sunday, June 3, 2018

In two words, how do you feel right now?

_____   _____

What are you grateful for today?

_____

_____

A goal you can accomplish today or get closer to:

_____

_____

What happened this week you want to remember:

_____

_____

How are you exactly the same as everyone else?

_____

Reflections

Note the highlights in your life in this moment.
Write down a quote that motivates you,
the titles of books you want to read
or documentaries to watch,
and a reason to smile
right now.

_____

_____

_____

_____

_____

_____

_____

_____

_____

Monday, June 4, 2018

In two words, how do you feel right now?

_____   _____

What are you grateful for today?

_____

_____

What are you looking forward to today?

_____

_____

A healthy habit you can start as of right now:

_____

_____

A friend you can send a letter to today:

_____

Tuesday, June 5, 2018

In two words, how do you feel right now?

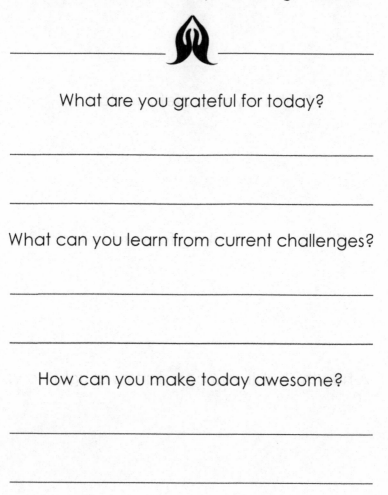

_____   _____

What are you grateful for today?

_____

_____

What can you learn from current challenges?

_____

_____

How can you make today awesome?

_____

_____

What physical ability are you grateful for today?

_____

Wednesday, June 6, 2018

In two words, how do you feel right now?

_____   _____

What are you grateful for today?

_____

_____

What would you like to do more often?

_____

_____

What would you like to do less often?

_____

_____

Modern technology you appreciate today:

_____

Thursday, June 7, 2018

In two words, how do you feel right now?

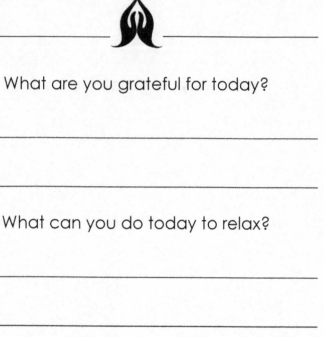

What are you grateful for today?

_____

_____

What can you do today to relax?

_____

_____

What is your priority today?

_____

_____

What skill are you most grateful for right now?

_____

Friday, June 8, 2018

In two words, how do you feel right now?

_____   _____

What are you grateful for today?

_____

_____

What do you have plenty of?

_____

_____

What piece of wisdom are you grateful for?

_____

_____

Which current relationship are you grateful for?

_____

Saturday, June 9, 2018

In two words, how do you feel right now?

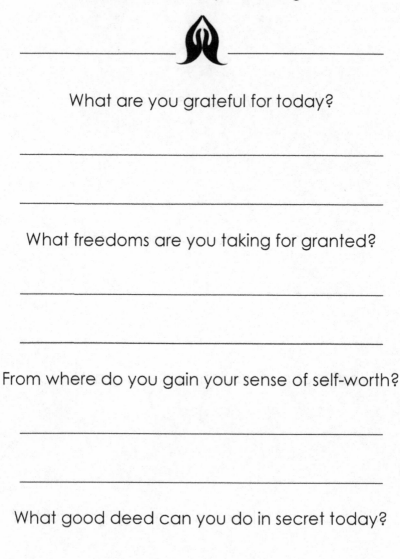

_____   _____

What are you grateful for today?

_____

_____

What freedoms are you taking for granted?

_____

_____

From where do you gain your sense of self-worth?

_____

_____

What good deed can you do in secret today?

_____

Sunday, June 10, 2018

In two words, how do you feel right now?

_____ — _____

What are you grateful for today?

_____

_____

A goal you can accomplish today or get closer to:

_____

_____

What happened this week you want to remember:

_____

_____

How are you exactly the same as everyone else?

_____

Reflections

Note the highlights in your life in this moment.
Write down a quote that motivates you,
the titles of books you want to read
or documentaries to watch,
and a reason to smile
right now.

_____

_____

_____

_____

_____

_____

_____

_____

Monday, June 11, 2018

In two words, how do you feel right now?

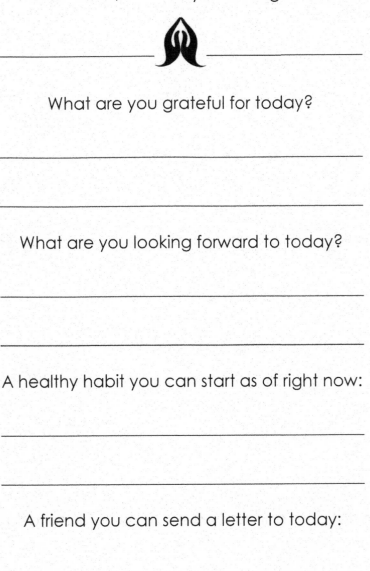

_____   _____

What are you grateful for today?

_____

_____

What are you looking forward to today?

_____

_____

A healthy habit you can start as of right now:

_____

_____

A friend you can send a letter to today:

_____

Tuesday, June 12, 2018

In two words, how do you feel right now?

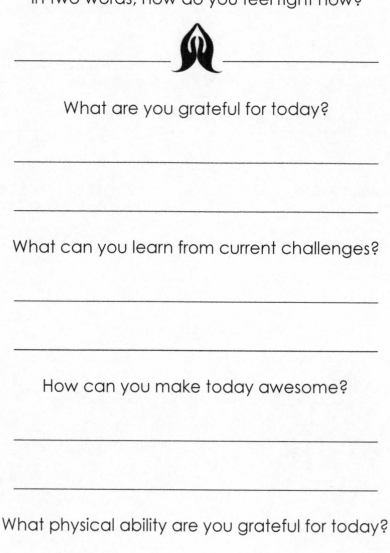

_____   _____

What are you grateful for today?

_____

_____

What can you learn from current challenges?

_____

_____

How can you make today awesome?

_____

_____

What physical ability are you grateful for today?

_____

Wednesday, June 13, 2018

In two words, how do you feel right now?

_____   _____

What are you grateful for today?

_____

_____

What would you like to do more often?

_____

_____

What would you like to do less often?

_____

_____

Modern technology you appreciate today:

_____

Thursday, June 14, 2018

In two words, how do you feel right now?

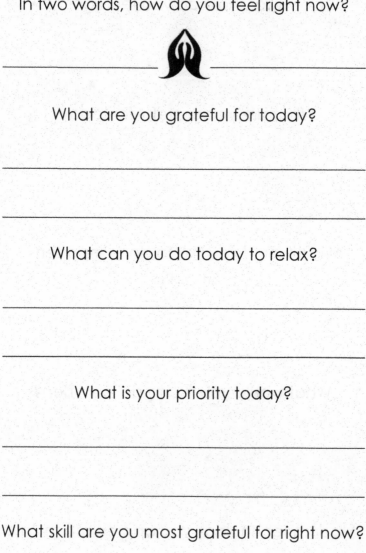

_____   _____

What are you grateful for today?

_____

_____

What can you do today to relax?

_____

_____

What is your priority today?

_____

_____

What skill are you most grateful for right now?

_____

Friday, June 15, 2018

In two words, how do you feel right now?

_____ _____

What are you grateful for today?

_____

_____

What do you have plenty of?

_____

_____

What piece of wisdom are you grateful for?

_____

_____

Which current relationship are you grateful for?

_____

Saturday, June 16, 2018

In two words, how do you feel right now?

_____ _____

What are you grateful for today?

_____

_____

What freedoms are you taking for granted?

_____

_____

From where do you gain your sense of self-worth?

_____

_____

What good deed can you do in secret today?

_____

Sunday, June 17, 2018

In two words, how do you feel right now?

_____ _____

What are you grateful for today?

_____

_____

A goal you can accomplish today or get closer to:

_____

_____

What happened this week you want to remember:

_____

_____

How are you exactly the same as everyone else?

_____

Reflections

Note the highlights in your life in this moment.
Write down a quote that motivates you,
the titles of books you want to read
or documentaries to watch,
and a reason to smile
right now.

_____

_____

_____

_____

_____

_____

_____

_____

Monday, June 18, 2018

In two words, how do you feel right now?

_____   _____

What are you grateful for today?

_____

_____

What are you looking forward to today?

_____

_____

A healthy habit you can start as of right now:

_____

_____

A friend you can send a letter to today:

_____

Tuesday, June 19, 2018

In two words, how do you feel right now?

_____   _____

What are you grateful for today?

_____

_____

What can you learn from current challenges?

_____

_____

How can you make today awesome?

_____

_____

What physical ability are you grateful for today?

_____

Wednesday, June 20, 2018

In two words, how do you feel right now?

_____   _____

What are you grateful for today?

_____

_____

What would you like to do more often?

_____

_____

What would you like to do less often?

_____

_____

Modern technology you appreciate today:

_____

Thursday, June 21, 2018

In two words, how do you feel right now?

_____   _____

What are you grateful for today?

_____

_____

What can you do today to relax?

_____

_____

What is your priority today?

_____

_____

What skill are you most grateful for right now?

_____

Friday, June 22, 2018

In two words, how do you feel right now?

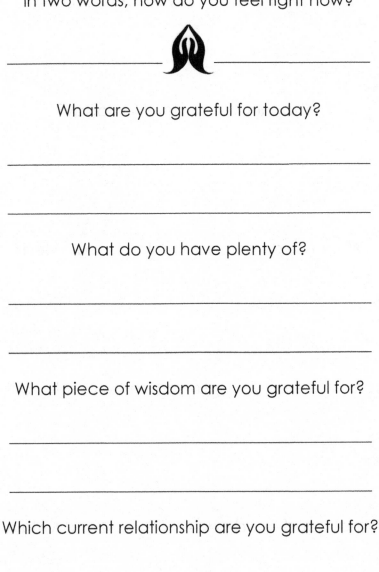

_____   _____

What are you grateful for today?

_____

_____

What do you have plenty of?

_____

_____

What piece of wisdom are you grateful for?

_____

_____

Which current relationship are you grateful for?

_____

Saturday, June 23, 2018

In two words, how do you feel right now?

_____ ∙ _____

What are you grateful for today?

_____

_____

What freedoms are you taking for granted?

_____

_____

From where do you gain your sense of self-worth?

_____

_____

What good deed can you do in secret today?

_____

Sunday, June 24, 2018

In two words, how do you feel right now?

_____ _____

What are you grateful for today?

_____

_____

A goal you can accomplish today or get closer to:

_____

_____

What happened this week you want to remember:

_____

_____

How are you exactly the same as everyone else?

_____

Reflections

Note the highlights in your life in this moment.
Write down a quote that motivates you,
the titles of books you want to read
or documentaries to watch,
and a reason to smile
right now.

_____

_____

_____

_____

_____

_____

_____

_____

_____

Monday, June 25, 2018

In two words, how do you feel right now?

_____ — _____

What are you grateful for today?

_____

_____

What are you looking forward to today?

_____

_____

A healthy habit you can start as of right now:

_____

_____

A friend you can send a letter to today:

_____

Tuesday, June 26, 2018

In two words, how do you feel right now?

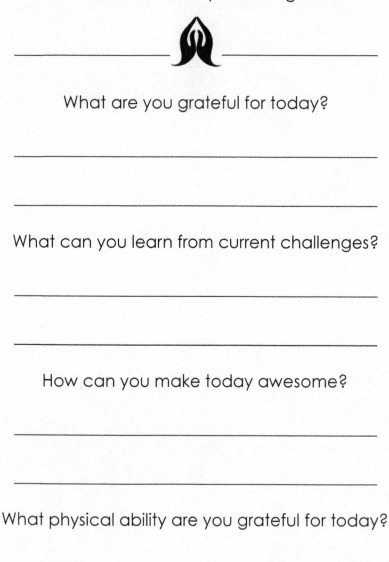

_____   _____

What are you grateful for today?

_____

_____

What can you learn from current challenges?

_____

_____

How can you make today awesome?

_____

_____

What physical ability are you grateful for today?

_____

Wednesday, June 27, 2018

In two words, how do you feel right now?

_____ _____

What are you grateful for today?

_____

_____

What would you like to do more often?

_____

_____

What would you like to do less often?

_____

_____

Modern technology you appreciate today:

_____

Thursday, June 28, 2018

In two words, how do you feel right now?

Mad _Angrey_

What are you grateful for today?

Go,

What can you do today to relax?

What is your priority today?

What skill are you most grateful for right now?

Friday, June 29, 2018

In two words, how do you feel right now?

_____ ✹ _____

What are you grateful for today?

_____

_____

What do you have plenty of?

_____

_____

What piece of wisdom are you grateful for?

_____

_____

Which current relationship are you grateful for?

_____

Saturday, June 30, 2018

In two words, how do you feel right now?

_____

What are you grateful for today?

_____

_____

What freedoms are you taking for granted?

_____

_____

From where do you gain your sense of self-worth?

_____

_____

What good deed can you do in secret today?

_____

Sunday, July 1, 2018

In two words, how do you feel right now?

_____ _____

What are you grateful for today?

_____

_____

A goal you can accomplish today or get closer to:

_____

_____

What happened this week you want to remember:

_____

_____

How are you exactly the same as everyone else?

_____

Reflections

Note the highlights in your life in this moment.
Write down a quote that motivates you,
the titles of books you want to read
or documentaries to watch,
and a reason to smile
right now.

_____

_____

_____

_____

_____

_____

_____

_____

_____

Monday, July 2, 2018

In two words, how do you feel right now?

_____   _____

What are you grateful for today?

_____

_____

What are you looking forward to today?

_____

_____

A healthy habit you can start as of right now:

_____

_____

A friend you can send a letter to today:

_____

Tuesday, July 3, 2018

In two words, how do you feel right now?

_____ _____

What are you grateful for today?

_____

_____

What can you learn from current challenges?

_____

_____

How can you make today awesome?

_____

_____

What physical ability are you grateful for today?

_____

Wednesday, July 4, 2018

In two words, how do you feel right now?

_____   _____

What are you grateful for today?

_____

_____

What would you like to do more often?

_____

_____

What would you like to do less often?

_____

_____

Modern technology you appreciate today:

_____

Thursday, July 5, 2018

In two words, how do you feel right now?

_____ _____

What are you grateful for today?

_____

_____

What can you do today to relax?

_____

_____

What is your priority today?

_____

_____

What skill are you most grateful for right now?

_____

Friday, July 6, 2018

In two words, how do you feel right now?

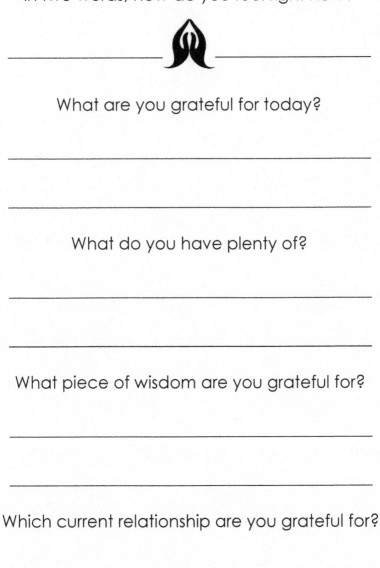

What are you grateful for today?

_____

_____

What do you have plenty of?

_____

_____

What piece of wisdom are you grateful for?

_____

_____

Which current relationship are you grateful for?

_____

Saturday, July 7, 2018

In two words, how do you feel right now?

_____   _____

What are you grateful for today?

_____

_____

What freedoms are you taking for granted?

_____

_____

From where do you gain your sense of self-worth?

_____

_____

What good deed can you do in secret today?

_____

Sunday, July 8, 2018

In two words, how do you feel right now?

_____   _____

What are you grateful for today?

_____

_____

A goal you can accomplish today or get closer to:

_____

_____

What happened this week you want to remember:

_____

_____

How are you exactly the same as everyone else?

_____

Reflections

Note the highlights in your life in this moment.
Write down a quote that motivates you,
the titles of books you want to read
or documentaries to watch,
and a reason to smile
right now.

_____

_____

_____

_____

_____

_____

_____

_____

Monday, July 9, 2018

In two words, how do you feel right now?

_____   _____

What are you grateful for today?

_____

_____

What are you looking forward to today?

_____

_____

A healthy habit you can start as of right now:

_____

_____

A friend you can send a letter to today:

_____

Tuesday, July 10, 2018

In two words, how do you feel right now?

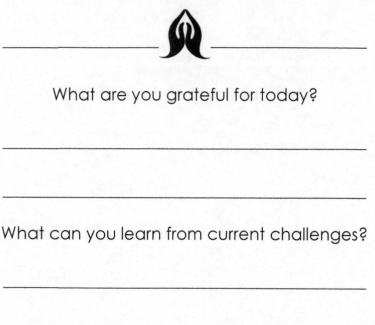

_____ _____

What are you grateful for today?

_____

_____

What can you learn from current challenges?

_____

_____

How can you make today awesome?

_____

_____

What physical ability are you grateful for today?

_____

Wednesday, July 11, 2018

In two words, how do you feel right now?

_____ _____

What are you grateful for today?

_____

_____

What would you like to do more often?

_____

_____

What would you like to do less often?

_____

_____

Modern technology you appreciate today:

_____

Thursday, July 12, 2018

In two words, how do you feel right now?

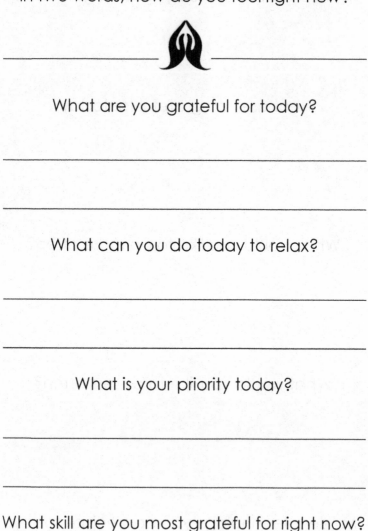

_____   _____

What are you grateful for today?

_____

_____

What can you do today to relax?

_____

_____

What is your priority today?

_____

_____

What skill are you most grateful for right now?

_____

Friday, July 13, 2018

In two words, how do you feel right now?

_____   _____

What are you grateful for today?

_____

_____

What do you have plenty of?

_____

_____

What piece of wisdom are you grateful for?

_____

_____

Which current relationship are you grateful for?

_____

Saturday, July 14, 2018

In two words, how do you feel right now?

_____ ꙮ _____

What are you grateful for today?

_____

_____

What freedoms are you taking for granted?

_____

_____

From where do you gain your sense of self-worth?

_____

_____

What good deed can you do in secret today?

_____

Sunday, July 15, 2018

In two words, how do you feel right now?

_____   _____

What are you grateful for today?

_____

_____

A goal you can accomplish today or get closer to:

_____

_____

What happened this week you want to remember:

_____

_____

How are you exactly the same as everyone else?

_____

Reflections

Note the highlights in your life in this moment.
Write down a quote that motivates you,
the titles of books you want to read
or documentaries to watch,
and a reason to smile
right now.

_____

_____

_____

_____

_____

_____

_____

_____

_____

Monday, July 16, 2018

In two words, how do you feel right now?

_____   _____

What are you grateful for today?

_____

_____

What are you looking forward to today?

_____

_____

A healthy habit you can start as of right now:

_____

_____

A friend you can send a letter to today:

_____

Tuesday, July 17, 2018

In two words, how do you feel right now?

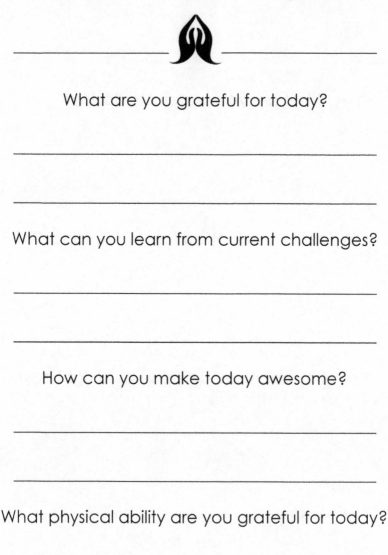

_____   _____

What are you grateful for today?

_____

_____

What can you learn from current challenges?

_____

_____

How can you make today awesome?

_____

_____

What physical ability are you grateful for today?

_____

Wednesday, July 18, 2018

In two words, how do you feel right now?

_____   _____

What are you grateful for today?

_____

_____

What would you like to do more often?

_____

_____

What would you like to do less often?

_____

_____

Modern technology you appreciate today:

_____

Thursday, July 19, 2018

In two words, how do you feel right now?

_____ _____

What are you grateful for today?

_____

_____

What can you do today to relax?

_____

_____

What is your priority today?

_____

_____

What skill are you most grateful for right now?

_____

Friday, July 20, 2018

In two words, how do you feel right now?

_____   _____

What are you grateful for today?

_____

_____

What do you have plenty of?

_____

_____

What piece of wisdom are you grateful for?

_____

_____

Which current relationship are you grateful for?

_____

Saturday, July 21, 2018

In two words, how do you feel right now?

_____   _____

What are you grateful for today?

_____

_____

What freedoms are you taking for granted?

_____

_____

From where do you gain your sense of self-worth?

_____

_____

What good deed can you do in secret today?

_____

Sunday, July 22, 2018

In two words, how do you feel right now?

_____ _____

What are you grateful for today?

_____

_____

A goal you can accomplish today or get closer to:

_____

_____

What happened this week you want to remember:

_____

_____

How are you exactly the same as everyone else?

_____

Reflections

Note the highlights in your life in this moment.
Write down a quote that motivates you,
the titles of books you want to read
or documentaries to watch,
and a reason to smile
right now.

Monday, July 23, 2018

In two words, how do you feel right now?

_____   _____

What are you grateful for today?

_____

_____

What are you looking forward to today?

_____

_____

A healthy habit you can start as of right now:

_____

_____

A friend you can send a letter to today:

_____

Tuesday, July 24, 2018

In two words, how do you feel right now?

_____   _____

What are you grateful for today?

_____

_____

What can you learn from current challenges?

_____

_____

How can you make today awesome?

_____

_____

What physical ability are you grateful for today?

_____

Wednesday, July 25, 2018

In two words, how do you feel right now?

_____   _____

What are you grateful for today?

_____

_____

What would you like to do more often?

_____

_____

What would you like to do less often?

_____

_____

Modern technology you appreciate today:

_____

Thursday, July 26, 2018

In two words, how do you feel right now?

_____

What are you grateful for today?

_____

_____

What can you do today to relax?

_____

_____

What is your priority today?

_____

_____

What skill are you most grateful for right now?

_____

Friday, July 27, 2018

In two words, how do you feel right now?

_____ _____

What are you grateful for today?

_____

_____

What do you have plenty of?

_____

_____

What piece of wisdom are you grateful for?

_____

_____

Which current relationship are you grateful for?

_____

Saturday, July 28, 2018

In two words, how do you feel right now?

_____   _____

What are you grateful for today?

_____

_____

What freedoms are you taking for granted?

_____

_____

From where do you gain your sense of self-worth?

_____

_____

What good deed can you do in secret today?

_____

Sunday, July 29, 2018

In two words, how do you feel right now?

_____ _____

What are you grateful for today?

_____

_____

A goal you can accomplish today or get closer to:

_____

_____

What happened this week you want to remember:

_____

_____

How are you exactly the same as everyone else?

_____

Reflections

Note the highlights in your life in this moment.
Write down a quote that motivates you,
the titles of books you want to read
or documentaries to watch,
and a reason to smile
right now.

_____

_____

_____

_____

_____

_____

_____

_____

_____

Monday, July 30, 2018

In two words, how do you feel right now?

_____   _____

What are you grateful for today?

_____

_____

What are you looking forward to today?

_____

_____

A healthy habit you can start as of right now:

_____

_____

A friend you can send a letter to today:

_____

Tuesday, July 31, 2018

In two words, how do you feel right now?

Happy _awsomme_

What are you grateful for today?

What can you learn from current challenges?

How can you make today awesome?

What physical ability are you grateful for today?

Wednesday, August 1, 2018

In two words, how do you feel right now?

_____   _____

What are you grateful for today?

_____

_____

What would you like to do more often?

_____

_____

What would you like to do less often?

_____

_____

Modern technology you appreciate today:

_____

Thursday, August 2, 2018

In two words, how do you feel right now?

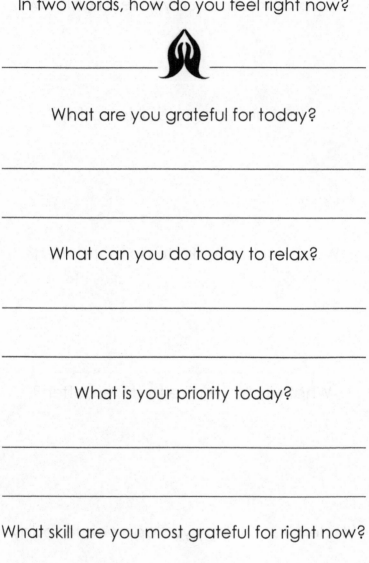

_____   _____

What are you grateful for today?

_____

_____

What can you do today to relax?

_____

_____

What is your priority today?

_____

_____

What skill are you most grateful for right now?

_____

Friday, August 3, 2018

In two words, how do you feel right now?

_____ _____

What are you grateful for today?

_____

_____

What do you have plenty of?

_____

_____

What piece of wisdom are you grateful for?

_____

_____

Which current relationship are you grateful for?

_____

Saturday, August 4, 2018

In two words, how do you feel right now?

_____ _____

What are you grateful for today?

_____

_____

What freedoms are you taking for granted?

_____

_____

From where do you gain your sense of self-worth?

_____

_____

What good deed can you do in secret today?

_____

Sunday, August 5, 2018

In two words, how do you feel right now?

_____ _____

What are you grateful for today?

_____

_____

A goal you can accomplish today or get closer to:

_____

_____

What happened this week you want to remember:

_____

_____

How are you exactly the same as everyone else?

_____

Reflections

Note the highlights in your life in this moment.
Write down a quote that motivates you,
the titles of books you want to read
or documentaries to watch,
and a reason to smile
right now.

_____

_____

_____

_____

_____

_____

_____

_____

_____

Monday, August 6, 2018

In two words, how do you feel right now?

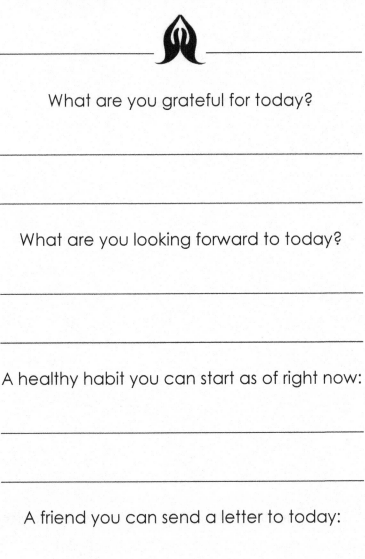

_____   _____

What are you grateful for today?

_____

_____

What are you looking forward to today?

_____

_____

A healthy habit you can start as of right now:

_____

_____

A friend you can send a letter to today:

_____

Tuesday, August 7, 2018

In two words, how do you feel right now?

_____ _____

What are you grateful for today?

_____

_____

What can you learn from current challenges?

_____

_____

How can you make today awesome?

_____

_____

What physical ability are you grateful for today?

_____

Wednesday, August 8, 2018

In two words, how do you feel right now?

_____   _____

What are you grateful for today?

_____

_____

What would you like to do more often?

_____

_____

What would you like to do less often?

_____

_____

Modern technology you appreciate today:

_____

Thursday, August 9, 2018

In two words, how do you feel right now?

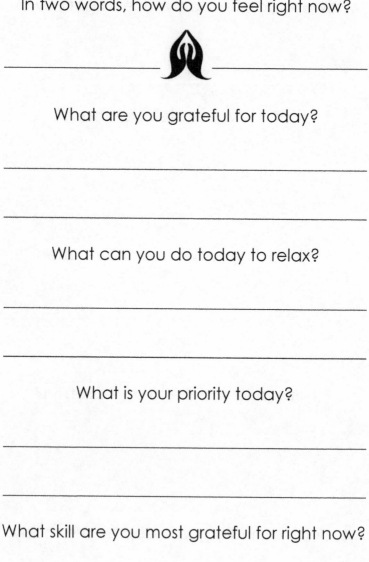

_____   _____

What are you grateful for today?

_____

_____

What can you do today to relax?

_____

_____

What is your priority today?

_____

_____

What skill are you most grateful for right now?

_____

Friday, August 10, 2018

In two words, how do you feel right now?

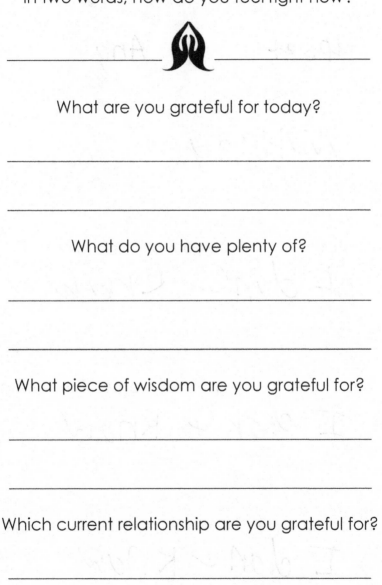

_____   _____

What are you grateful for today?

_____

_____

What do you have plenty of?

_____

_____

What piece of wisdom are you grateful for?

_____

_____

Which current relationship are you grateful for?

_____

Saturday, August 11, 2018

In two words, how do you feel right now?

upset ___ Angy

What are you grateful for today?

Nothing

What freedoms are you taking for granted?

I don't know

From where do you gain your sense of self-worth?

I don't know

What good deed can you do in secret today?

I don't know

Sunday, August 12, 2018

In two words, how do you feel right now?

_____ _____

What are you grateful for today?

_____

_____

A goal you can accomplish today or get closer to:

_____

_____

What happened this week you want to remember:

_____

_____

How are you exactly the same as everyone else?

_____

Reflections

Note the highlights in your life in this moment.
Write down a quote that motivates you,
the titles of books you want to read
or documentaries to watch,
and a reason to smile
right now.

_____

_____

_____

_____

_____

_____

_____

_____

_____

Monday, August 13, 2018

In two words, how do you feel right now?

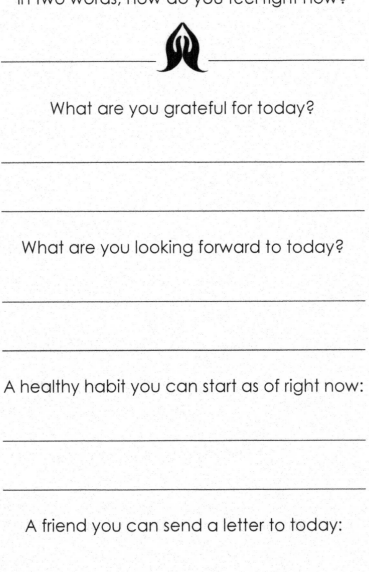

_____ _____

What are you grateful for today?

_____

_____

What are you looking forward to today?

_____

_____

A healthy habit you can start as of right now:

_____

_____

A friend you can send a letter to today:

_____

Tuesday, August 14, 2018

In two words, how do you feel right now?

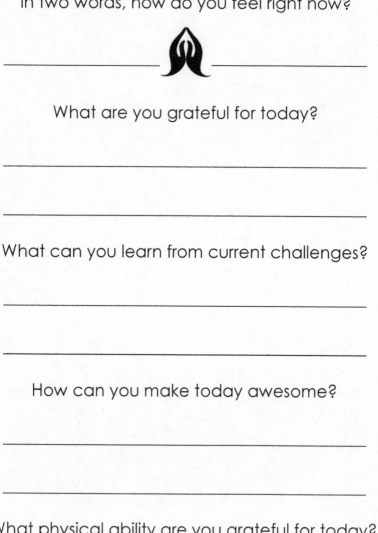

_____   _____

What are you grateful for today?

_____

_____

What can you learn from current challenges?

_____

_____

How can you make today awesome?

_____

_____

What physical ability are you grateful for today?

_____

Wednesday, August 15, 2018

In two words, how do you feel right now?

_____   _____

What are you grateful for today?

_____

_____

What would you like to do more often?

_____

_____

What would you like to do less often?

_____

_____

Modern technology you appreciate today:

_____

Thursday, August 16, 2018

In two words, how do you feel right now?

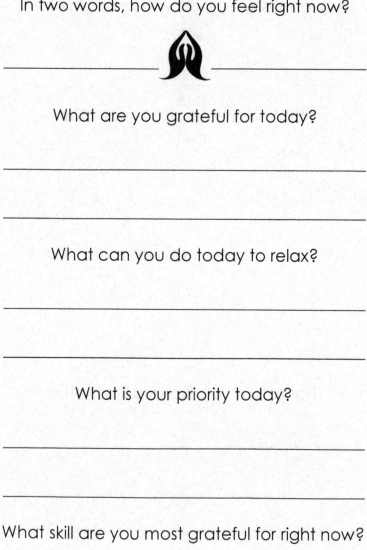

_____   _____

What are you grateful for today?

_____

_____

What can you do today to relax?

_____

_____

What is your priority today?

_____

_____

What skill are you most grateful for right now?

_____

Friday, August 17, 2018

In two words, how do you feel right now?

_____   _____

What are you grateful for today?

_____

_____

What do you have plenty of?

_____

_____

What piece of wisdom are you grateful for?

_____

_____

Which current relationship are you grateful for?

_____

Saturday, August 18, 2018

In two words, how do you feel right now?

_____ _____

What are you grateful for today?

_____

_____

What freedoms are you taking for granted?

_____

_____

From where do you gain your sense of self-worth?

_____

_____

What good deed can you do in secret today?

_____

Sunday, August 19, 2018

In two words, how do you feel right now?

_____ _____

What are you grateful for today?

_____

_____

A goal you can accomplish today or get closer to:

_____

_____

What happened this week you want to remember:

_____

_____

How are you exactly the same as everyone else?

_____

Reflections

Note the highlights in your life in this moment.
Write down a quote that motivates you,
the titles of books you want to read
or documentaries to watch,
and a reason to smile
right now.

_____

_____

_____

_____

_____

_____

_____

_____

_____

Monday, August 20, 2018

In two words, how do you feel right now?

_____   _____

What are you grateful for today?

_____

_____

What are you looking forward to today?

_____

_____

A healthy habit you can start as of right now:

_____

_____

A friend you can send a letter to today:

_____

Tuesday, August 21, 2018

In two words, how do you feel right now?

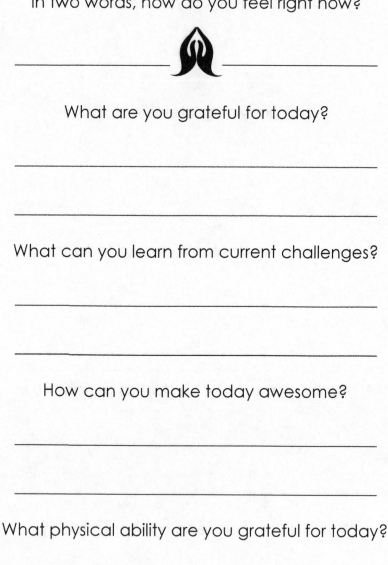

_____   _____

What are you grateful for today?

_____

_____

What can you learn from current challenges?

_____

_____

How can you make today awesome?

_____

_____

What physical ability are you grateful for today?

_____

Wednesday, August 22, 2018

In two words, how do you feel right now?

_____ _____

What are you grateful for today?

_____

_____

What would you like to do more often?

_____

_____

What would you like to do less often?

_____

_____

Modern technology you appreciate today:

_____

Thursday, August 23, 2018

In two words, how do you feel right now?

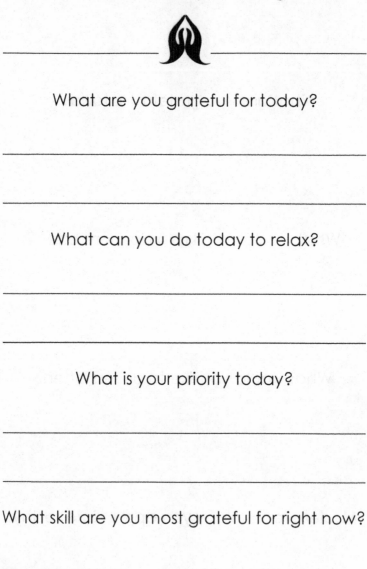

_____   _____

What are you grateful for today?

_____

_____

What can you do today to relax?

_____

_____

What is your priority today?

_____

_____

What skill are you most grateful for right now?

_____

Friday, August 24, 2018

In two words, how do you feel right now?

_____   _____

What are you grateful for today?

_____

_____

What do you have plenty of?

_____

_____

What piece of wisdom are you grateful for?

_____

_____

Which current relationship are you grateful for?

_____

Saturday, August 25, 2018

In two words, how do you feel right now?

_____ ⚛ _____

What are you grateful for today?

_____

_____

What freedoms are you taking for granted?

_____

_____

From where do you gain your sense of self-worth?

_____

_____

What good deed can you do in secret today?

_____

Sunday, August 26, 2018

In two words, how do you feel right now?

_____   _____

What are you grateful for today?

_____

_____

A goal you can accomplish today or get closer to:

_____

_____

What happened this week you want to remember:

_____

_____

How are you exactly the same as everyone else?

_____

Reflections

Note the highlights in your life in this moment.
Write down a quote that motivates you,
the titles of books you want to read
or documentaries to watch,
and a reason to smile
right now.

_____

_____

_____

_____

_____

_____

_____

_____

Monday, August 27, 2018

In two words, how do you feel right now?

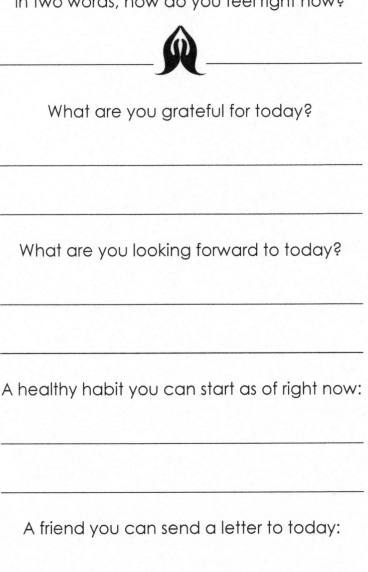

_____ _____

What are you grateful for today?

_____

_____

What are you looking forward to today?

_____

_____

A healthy habit you can start as of right now:

_____

_____

A friend you can send a letter to today:

_____

Tuesday, August 28, 2018

In two words, how do you feel right now?

_____ _____

What are you grateful for today?

_____

_____

What can you learn from current challenges?

_____

_____

How can you make today awesome?

_____

_____

What physical ability are you grateful for today?

_____

Wednesday, August 29, 2018

In two words, how do you feel right now?

_____   —   _____

What are you grateful for today?

_____

_____

What would you like to do more often?

_____

_____

What would you like to do less often?

_____

_____

Modern technology you appreciate today:

_____

Thursday, August 30, 2018

In two words, how do you feel right now?

_____   _____

What are you grateful for today?

_____

_____

What can you do today to relax?

_____

_____

What is your priority today?

_____

_____

What skill are you most grateful for right now?

_____

Friday, August 31, 2018

In two words, how do you feel right now?

_____ _____

What are you grateful for today?

_____

_____

What do you have plenty of?

_____

_____

What piece of wisdom are you grateful for?

_____

_____

Which current relationship are you grateful for?

_____

Saturday, September 1, 2018

In two words, how do you feel right now?

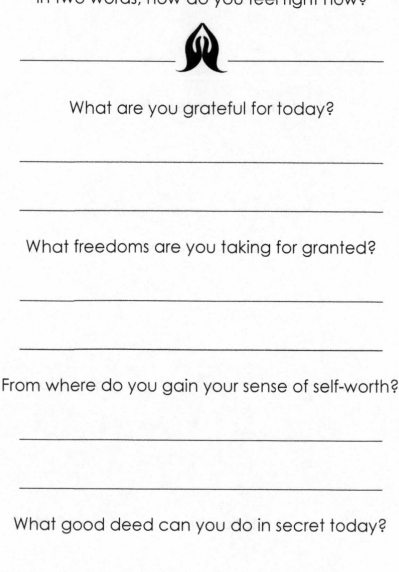

_____   _____

What are you grateful for today?

_____

_____

What freedoms are you taking for granted?

_____

_____

From where do you gain your sense of self-worth?

_____

_____

What good deed can you do in secret today?

_____

Sunday, September 2, 2018

In two words, how do you feel right now?

_____ 🙏 _____

What are you grateful for today?

_____

_____

A goal you can accomplish today or get closer to:

_____

_____

What happened this week you want to remember:

_____

_____

How are you exactly the same as everyone else?

_____

Reflections

Note the highlights in your life in this moment.
Write down a quote that motivates you,
the titles of books you want to read
or documentaries to watch,
and a reason to smile
right now.

_____

_____

_____

_____

_____

_____

_____

_____

_____

Monday, September 3, 2018

In two words, how do you feel right now?

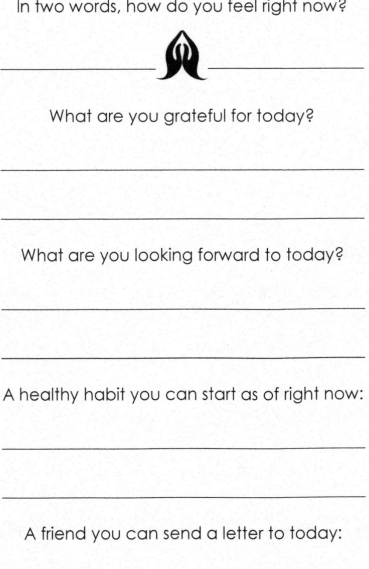

_____   _____

What are you grateful for today?

_____

_____

What are you looking forward to today?

_____

_____

A healthy habit you can start as of right now:

_____

_____

A friend you can send a letter to today:

_____

Tuesday, September 4, 2018

In two words, how do you feel right now?

_____ _____

What are you grateful for today?

_____

_____

What can you learn from current challenges?

_____

_____

How can you make today awesome?

_____

_____

What physical ability are you grateful for today?

_____

Wednesday, September 5, 2018

In two words, how do you feel right now?

_____ _____

What are you grateful for today?

_____

_____

What would you like to do more often?

_____

_____

What would you like to do less often?

_____

_____

Modern technology you appreciate today:

_____

Thursday, September 6, 2018

In two words, how do you feel right now?

_____ — _____

What are you grateful for today?

_____

_____

What can you do today to relax?

_____

_____

What is your priority today?

_____

_____

What skill are you most grateful for right now?

_____

Friday, September 7, 2018

In two words, how do you feel right now?

_____   _____

What are you grateful for today?

_____

_____

What do you have plenty of?

_____

_____

What piece of wisdom are you grateful for?

_____

_____

Which current relationship are you grateful for?

_____

Saturday, September 8, 2018

In two words, how do you feel right now?

_____   _____

What are you grateful for today?

_____

_____

What freedoms are you taking for granted?

_____

_____

From where do you gain your sense of self-worth?

_____

_____

What good deed can you do in secret today?

_____

Sunday, September 9, 2018

In two words, how do you feel right now?

_____ _____

What are you grateful for today?

_____

_____

A goal you can accomplish today or get closer to:

_____

_____

What happened this week you want to remember:

_____

_____

How are you exactly the same as everyone else?

_____

Reflections

Note the highlights in your life in this moment.
Write down a quote that motivates you,
the titles of books you want to read
or documentaries to watch,
and a reason to smile
right now.

_____

_____

_____

_____

_____

_____

_____

_____

Monday, September 10, 2018

In two words, how do you feel right now?

_____   _____

What are you grateful for today?

_____

_____

What are you looking forward to today?

_____

_____

A healthy habit you can start as of right now:

_____

_____

A friend you can send a letter to today:

_____

Tuesday, September 11, 2018

In two words, how do you feel right now?

_____   _____

What are you grateful for today?

_____

_____

What can you learn from current challenges?

_____

_____

How can you make today awesome?

_____

_____

What physical ability are you grateful for today?

_____

Wednesday, September 12, 2018

In two words, how do you feel right now?

_____ _____

What are you grateful for today?

_____

_____

What would you like to do more often?

_____

_____

What would you like to do less often?

_____

_____

Modern technology you appreciate today:

_____

Thursday, September 13, 2018

In two words, how do you feel right now?

_____   _____

What are you grateful for today?

_____

_____

What can you do today to relax?

_____

_____

What is your priority today?

_____

_____

What skill are you most grateful for right now?

_____

Friday, September 14, 2018

In two words, how do you feel right now?

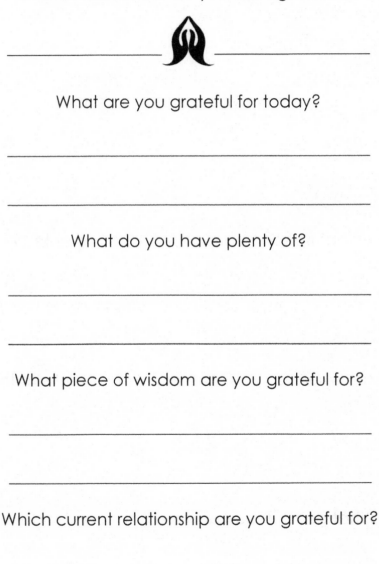

_____   _____

What are you grateful for today?

_____

_____

What do you have plenty of?

_____

_____

What piece of wisdom are you grateful for?

_____

_____

Which current relationship are you grateful for?

_____

Saturday, September 15, 2018

In two words, how do you feel right now?

_____ 🙏 _____

What are you grateful for today?

_____

_____

What freedoms are you taking for granted?

_____

_____

From where do you gain your sense of self-worth?

_____

_____

What good deed can you do in secret today?

_____

Sunday, September 16, 2018

In two words, how do you feel right now?

_____ _____

What are you grateful for today?

_____

_____

A goal you can accomplish today or get closer to:

_____

_____

What happened this week you want to remember:

_____

_____

How are you exactly the same as everyone else?

_____

Reflections

Note the highlights in your life in this moment.
Write down a quote that motivates you,
the titles of books you want to read
or documentaries to watch,
and a reason to smile
right now.

_____

_____

_____

_____

_____

_____

_____

_____

_____

Monday, September 17, 2018

In two words, how do you feel right now?

_____ _____

What are you grateful for today?

_____

_____

What are you looking forward to today?

_____

_____

A healthy habit you can start as of right now:

_____

_____

A friend you can send a letter to today:

_____

Tuesday, September 18, 2018

In two words, how do you feel right now?

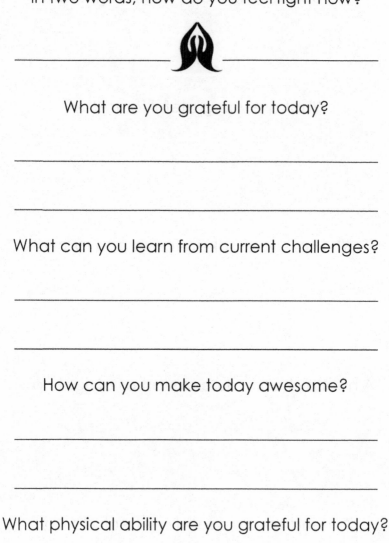

_____   _____

What are you grateful for today?

_____

_____

What can you learn from current challenges?

_____

_____

How can you make today awesome?

_____

_____

What physical ability are you grateful for today?

_____

September 18

Wednesday, September 19, 2018

In two words, how do you feel right now?

_____   _____

What are you grateful for today?

_____

_____

What would you like to do more often?

_____

_____

What would you like to do less often?

_____

_____

Modern technology you appreciate today:

_____

Thursday, September 20, 2018

In two words, how do you feel right now?

_____ _____

What are you grateful for today?

_____

_____

What can you do today to relax?

_____

_____

What is your priority today?

_____

_____

What skill are you most grateful for right now?

_____

Friday, September 21, 2018

In two words, how do you feel right now?

_____   _____

What are you grateful for today?

_____

_____

What do you have plenty of?

_____

_____

What piece of wisdom are you grateful for?

_____

_____

Which current relationship are you grateful for?

_____

Saturday, September 22, 2018

In two words, how do you feel right now?

_____   _____

What are you grateful for today?

_____

_____

What freedoms are you taking for granted?

_____

_____

From where do you gain your sense of self-worth?

_____

_____

What good deed can you do in secret today?

_____

Sunday, September 23, 2018

In two words, how do you feel right now?

_____ _____

What are you grateful for today?

_____

_____

A goal you can accomplish today or get closer to:

_____

_____

What happened this week you want to remember:

_____

_____

How are you exactly the same as everyone else?

_____

Reflections

Note the highlights in your life in this moment.
Write down a quote that motivates you,
the titles of books you want to read
or documentaries to watch,
and a reason to smile
right now.

_____

_____

_____

_____

_____

_____

_____

_____

_____

Monday, September 24, 2018

In two words, how do you feel right now?

_____   _____

What are you grateful for today?

_____

_____

What are you looking forward to today?

_____

_____

A healthy habit you can start as of right now:

_____

_____

A friend you can send a letter to today:

_____

Tuesday, September 25, 2018

In two words, how do you feel right now?

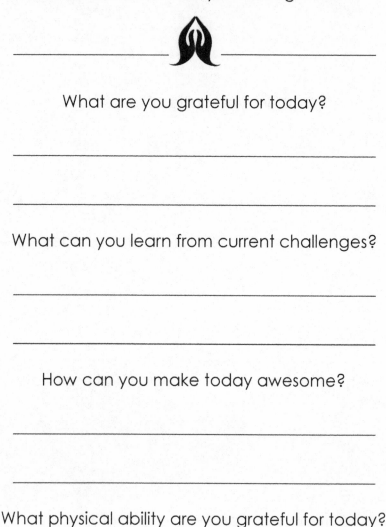

_____ _____

What are you grateful for today?

_____

_____

What can you learn from current challenges?

_____

_____

How can you make today awesome?

_____

_____

What physical ability are you grateful for today?

_____

Wednesday, September 26, 2018

In two words, how do you feel right now?

_____ _____

What are you grateful for today?

_____

_____

What would you like to do more often?

_____

_____

What would you like to do less often?

_____

_____

Modern technology you appreciate today:

_____

Thursday, September 27, 2018

In two words, how do you feel right now?

_____   _____

What are you grateful for today?

_____

_____

What can you do today to relax?

_____

_____

What is your priority today?

_____

_____

What skill are you most grateful for right now?

_____

Friday, September 28, 2018

In two words, how do you feel right now?

_____ _____

What are you grateful for today?

_____

_____

What do you have plenty of?

_____

_____

What piece of wisdom are you grateful for?

_____

_____

Which current relationship are you grateful for?

_____

Saturday, September 29, 2018

In two words, how do you feel right now?

——————————— ———————————

What are you grateful for today?

_____

_____

What freedoms are you taking for granted?

_____

_____

From where do you gain your sense of self-worth?

_____

_____

What good deed can you do in secret today?

_____

Sunday, September 30, 2018

In two words, how do you feel right now?

_____   _____

What are you grateful for today?

_____

_____

A goal you can accomplish today or get closer to:

_____

_____

What happened this week you want to remember:

_____

_____

How are you exactly the same as everyone else?

_____

Reflections

Note the highlights in your life in this moment.
Write down a quote that motivates you,
the titles of books you want to read
or documentaries to watch,
and a reason to smile
right now.

_____

_____

_____

_____

_____

_____

_____

_____

_____

Monday, October 1, 2018

In two words, how do you feel right now?

_____   _____

What are you grateful for today?

_____

_____

What are you looking forward to today?

_____

_____

A healthy habit you can start as of right now:

_____

_____

A friend you can send a letter to today:

_____

Tuesday, October 2, 2018

In two words, how do you feel right now?

_____   _____

What are you grateful for today?

_____

_____

What can you learn from current challenges?

_____

_____

How can you make today awesome?

_____

_____

What physical ability are you grateful for today?

_____

October 2

Wednesday, October 3, 2018

In two words, how do you feel right now?

_____ _____

What are you grateful for today?

_____

_____

What would you like to do more often?

_____

_____

What would you like to do less often?

_____

_____

Modern technology you appreciate today:

_____

Thursday, October 4, 2018

In two words, how do you feel right now?

_____ _____

What are you grateful for today?

_____

_____

What can you do today to relax?

_____

_____

What is your priority today?

_____

_____

What skill are you most grateful for right now?

_____

Friday, October 5, 2018

In two words, how do you feel right now?

_____ _____

What are you grateful for today?

_____

_____

What do you have plenty of?

_____

_____

What piece of wisdom are you grateful for?

_____

_____

Which current relationship are you grateful for?

_____

Saturday, October 6, 2018

In two words, how do you feel right now?

_____   _____

What are you grateful for today?

_____

_____

What freedoms are you taking for granted?

_____

_____

From where do you gain your sense of self-worth?

_____

_____

What good deed can you do in secret today?

_____

Sunday, October 7, 2018

In two words, how do you feel right now?

_____   _____

What are you grateful for today?

_____

_____

A goal you can accomplish today or get closer to:

_____

_____

What happened this week you want to remember:

_____

_____

How are you exactly the same as everyone else?

_____

Reflections

Note the highlights in your life in this moment.
Write down a quote that motivates you,
the titles of books you want to read
or documentaries to watch,
and a reason to smile
right now.

_____

_____

_____

_____

_____

_____

_____

_____

_____

Monday, October 8, 2018

In two words, how do you feel right now?

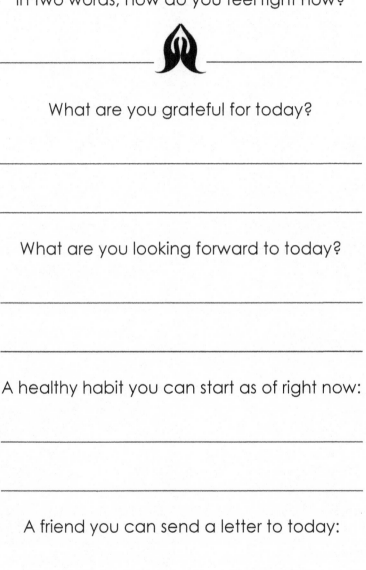

_____   _____

What are you grateful for today?

_____

_____

What are you looking forward to today?

_____

_____

A healthy habit you can start as of right now:

_____

_____

A friend you can send a letter to today:

_____

Tuesday, October 9, 2018

In two words, how do you feel right now?

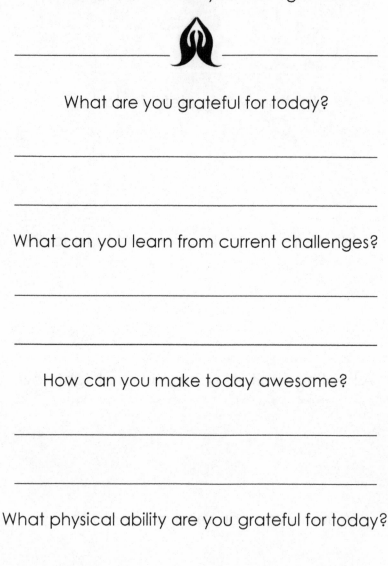

_____   _____

What are you grateful for today?

_____

_____

What can you learn from current challenges?

_____

_____

How can you make today awesome?

_____

_____

What physical ability are you grateful for today?

_____

Wednesday, October 10, 2018

In two words, how do you feel right now?

_____   _____

What are you grateful for today?

_____

_____

What would you like to do more often?

_____

_____

What would you like to do less often?

_____

_____

Modern technology you appreciate today:

_____

Thursday, October 11, 2018

In two words, how do you feel right now?

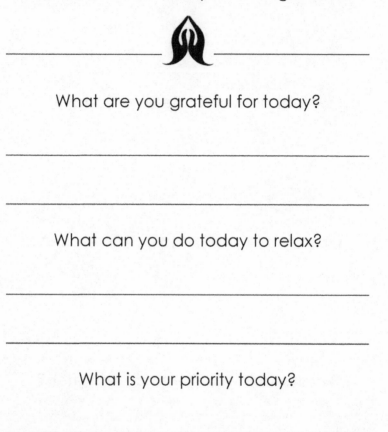

_____   _____

What are you grateful for today?

_____

_____

What can you do today to relax?

_____

_____

What is your priority today?

_____

_____

What skill are you most grateful for right now?

_____

October 11

Friday, October 12, 2018

In two words, how do you feel right now?

_____ _____

What are you grateful for today?

_____

_____

What do you have plenty of?

_____

_____

What piece of wisdom are you grateful for?

_____

_____

Which current relationship are you grateful for?

_____

Saturday, October 13, 2018

In two words, how do you feel right now?

_____ ✺ _____

What are you grateful for today?

_____

_____

What freedoms are you taking for granted?

_____

_____

From where do you gain your sense of self-worth?

_____

_____

What good deed can you do in secret today?

_____

October 13

Sunday, October 14, 2018

In two words, how do you feel right now?

_____ — _____

What are you grateful for today?

_____

_____

A goal you can accomplish today or get closer to:

_____

_____

What happened this week you want to remember:

_____

_____

How are you exactly the same as everyone else?

_____

Reflections

Note the highlights in your life in this moment.
Write down a quote that motivates you,
the titles of books you want to read
or documentaries to watch,
and a reason to smile
right now.

_____

_____

_____

_____

_____

_____

_____

_____

Monday, October 15, 2018

In two words, how do you feel right now?

_____   _____

What are you grateful for today?

_____

_____

What are you looking forward to today?

_____

_____

A healthy habit you can start as of right now:

_____

_____

A friend you can send a letter to today:

_____

Tuesday, October 16, 2018

In two words, how do you feel right now?

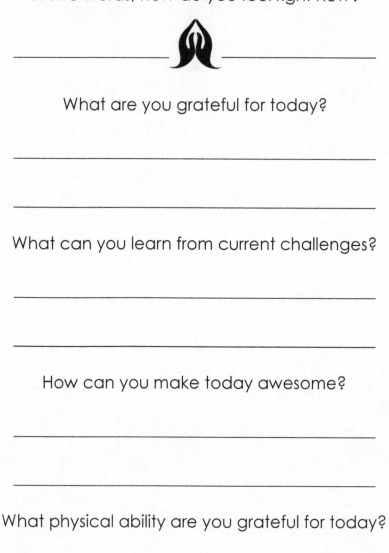

_____   _____

What are you grateful for today?

_____

_____

What can you learn from current challenges?

_____

_____

How can you make today awesome?

_____

_____

What physical ability are you grateful for today?

_____

October 16

Wednesday, October 17, 2018

In two words, how do you feel right now?

_____   _____

What are you grateful for today?

_____

_____

What would you like to do more often?

_____

_____

What would you like to do less often?

_____

_____

Modern technology you appreciate today:

_____

Thursday, October 18, 2018

In two words, how do you feel right now?

_____   _____

What are you grateful for today?

_____

_____

What can you do today to relax?

_____

_____

What is your priority today?

_____

_____

What skill are you most grateful for right now?

_____

Friday, October 19, 2018

In two words, how do you feel right now?

_____   _____

What are you grateful for today?

_____

_____

What do you have plenty of?

_____

_____

What piece of wisdom are you grateful for?

_____

_____

Which current relationship are you grateful for?

_____

Saturday, October 20, 2018

In two words, how do you feel right now?

_____ ⚜ _____

What are you grateful for today?

_____

_____

What freedoms are you taking for granted?

_____

_____

From where do you gain your sense of self-worth?

_____

_____

What good deed can you do in secret today?

_____

Sunday, October 21, 2018

In two words, how do you feel right now?

_____   _____

What are you grateful for today?

_____

_____

A goal you can accomplish today or get closer to:

_____

_____

What happened this week you want to remember:

_____

_____

How are you exactly the same as everyone else?

_____

Reflections

Note the highlights in your life in this moment.
Write down a quote that motivates you,
the titles of books you want to read
or documentaries to watch,
and a reason to smile
right now.

_____

_____

_____

_____

_____

_____

_____

_____

_____

Monday, October 22, 2018

In two words, how do you feel right now?

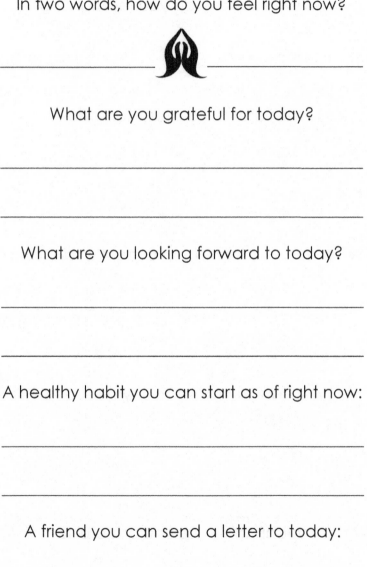

_____   _____

What are you grateful for today?

_____

_____

What are you looking forward to today?

_____

_____

A healthy habit you can start as of right now:

_____

_____

A friend you can send a letter to today:

_____

Tuesday, October 23, 2018

In two words, how do you feel right now?

_____   _____

What are you grateful for today?

_____

_____

What can you learn from current challenges?

_____

_____

How can you make today awesome?

_____

_____

What physical ability are you grateful for today?

_____

October 23

Wednesday, October 24, 2018

In two words, how do you feel right now?

_____   _____

What are you grateful for today?

_____

_____

What would you like to do more often?

_____

_____

What would you like to do less often?

_____

_____

Modern technology you appreciate today:

_____

Thursday, October 25, 2018

In two words, how do you feel right now?

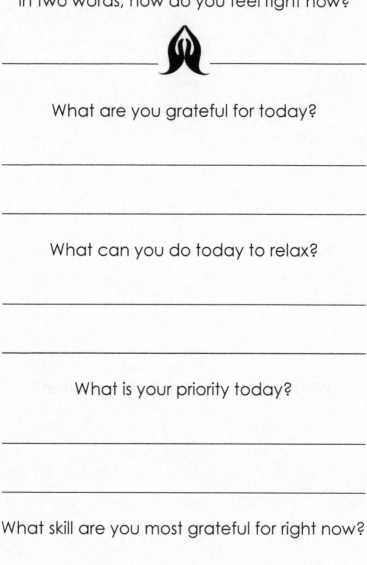

_____   _____

What are you grateful for today?

_____

_____

What can you do today to relax?

_____

_____

What is your priority today?

_____

_____

What skill are you most grateful for right now?

_____

Friday, October 26, 2018

In two words, how do you feel right now?

_____   _____

What are you grateful for today?

_____

_____

What do you have plenty of?

_____

_____

What piece of wisdom are you grateful for?

_____

_____

Which current relationship are you grateful for?

_____

Saturday, October 27, 2018

In two words, how do you feel right now?

_____ _____

What are you grateful for today?

_____

_____

What freedoms are you taking for granted?

_____

_____

From where do you gain your sense of self-worth?

_____

_____

What good deed can you do in secret today?

_____

Sunday, October 28, 2018

In two words, how do you feel right now?

_____ _____

What are you grateful for today?

_____

_____

A goal you can accomplish today or get closer to:

_____

_____

What happened this week you want to remember:

_____

_____

How are you exactly the same as everyone else?

_____

Reflections

Note the highlights in your life in this moment.
Write down a quote that motivates you,
the titles of books you want to read
or documentaries to watch,
and a reason to smile
right now.

_____

_____

_____

_____

_____

_____

_____

_____

Monday, October 29, 2018

In two words, how do you feel right now?

_____   _____

What are you grateful for today?

_____

_____

What are you looking forward to today?

_____

_____

A healthy habit you can start as of right now:

_____

_____

A friend you can send a letter to today:

_____

Tuesday, October 30, 2018

In two words, how do you feel right now?

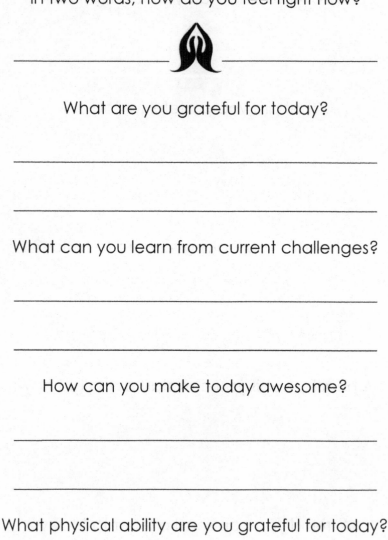

_____ ⚜ _____

What are you grateful for today?

_____

_____

What can you learn from current challenges?

_____

_____

How can you make today awesome?

_____

_____

What physical ability are you grateful for today?

_____

Wednesday, October 31, 2018

In two words, how do you feel right now?

———————————   ———————————

What are you grateful for today?

_____

_____

What would you like to do more often?

_____

_____

What would you like to do less often?

_____

_____

Modern technology you appreciate today:

_____

Thursday, November 1, 2018

In two words, how do you feel right now?

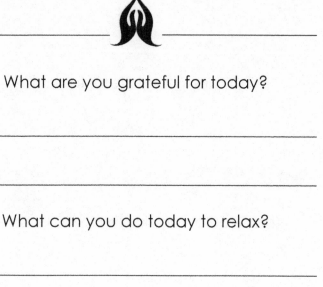

_____   _____

What are you grateful for today?

_____

_____

What can you do today to relax?

_____

_____

What is your priority today?

_____

_____

What skill are you most grateful for right now?

_____

Friday, November 2, 2018

In two words, how do you feel right now?

_____   _____

What are you grateful for today?

_____

_____

What do you have plenty of?

_____

_____

What piece of wisdom are you grateful for?

_____

_____

Which current relationship are you grateful for?

_____

Saturday, November 3, 2018

In two words, how do you feel right now?

_____ _____

What are you grateful for today?

_____

_____

What freedoms are you taking for granted?

_____

_____

From where do you gain your sense of self-worth?

_____

_____

What good deed can you do in secret today?

_____

Sunday, November 4, 2018

In two words, how do you feel right now?

_____   _____

What are you grateful for today?

_____

_____

A goal you can accomplish today or get closer to:

_____

_____

What happened this week you want to remember:

_____

_____

How are you exactly the same as everyone else?

_____

Reflections

Note the highlights in your life in this moment.
Write down a quote that motivates you,
the titles of books you want to read
or documentaries to watch,
and a reason to smile
right now.

_____

_____

_____

_____

_____

_____

_____

_____

_____

Monday, November 5, 2018

In two words, how do you feel right now?

_____   _____

What are you grateful for today?

_____

_____

What are you looking forward to today?

_____

_____

A healthy habit you can start as of right now:

_____

_____

A friend you can send a letter to today:

_____

Tuesday, November 6, 2018

In two words, how do you feel right now?

_____   _____

What are you grateful for today?

_____

_____

What can you learn from current challenges?

_____

_____

How can you make today awesome?

_____

_____

What physical ability are you grateful for today?

_____

Wednesday, November 7, 2018

In two words, how do you feel right now?

_____ _____

What are you grateful for today?

_____

_____

What would you like to do more often?

_____

_____

What would you like to do less often?

_____

_____

Modern technology you appreciate today:

_____

Thursday, November 8, 2018

In two words, how do you feel right now?

_____ _____

What are you grateful for today?

_____

_____

What can you do today to relax?

_____

_____

What is your priority today?

_____

_____

What skill are you most grateful for right now?

_____

Friday, November 9, 2018

In two words, how do you feel right now?

What are you grateful for today?

_____

_____

What do you have plenty of?

_____

_____

What piece of wisdom are you grateful for?

_____

_____

Which current relationship are you grateful for?

_____

Saturday, November 10, 2018

In two words, how do you feel right now?

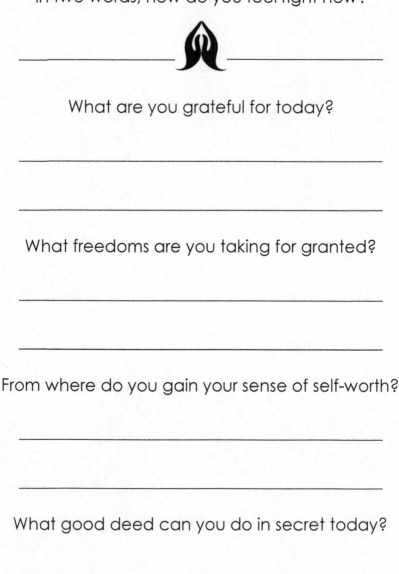

_____   _____

What are you grateful for today?

_____

_____

What freedoms are you taking for granted?

_____

_____

From where do you gain your sense of self-worth?

_____

_____

What good deed can you do in secret today?

_____

Sunday, November 11, 2018

In two words, how do you feel right now?

_____ _____

What are you grateful for today?

_____

_____

A goal you can accomplish today or get closer to:

_____

_____

What happened this week you want to remember:

_____

_____

How are you exactly the same as everyone else?

_____

Reflections

Note the highlights in your life in this moment.
Write down a quote that motivates you,
the titles of books you want to read
or documentaries to watch,
and a reason to smile
right now.

_____

_____

_____

_____

_____

_____

_____

_____

Monday, November 12, 2018

In two words, how do you feel right now?

_____   _____

What are you grateful for today?

_____

_____

What are you looking forward to today?

_____

_____

A healthy habit you can start as of right now:

_____

_____

A friend you can send a letter to today:

_____

Tuesday, November 13, 2018

In two words, how do you feel right now?

_____   _____

What are you grateful for today?

_____

_____

What can you learn from current challenges?

_____

_____

How can you make today awesome?

_____

_____

What physical ability are you grateful for today?

_____

Wednesday, November 14, 2018

In two words, how do you feel right now?

_____

What are you grateful for today?

_____

_____

What would you like to do more often?

_____

_____

What would you like to do less often?

_____

_____

Modern technology you appreciate today:

_____

Thursday, November 15, 2018

In two words, how do you feel right now?

_____   _____

What are you grateful for today?

_____

_____

What can you do today to relax?

_____

_____

What is your priority today?

_____

_____

What skill are you most grateful for right now?

_____

Friday, November 16, 2018

In two words, how do you feel right now?

_____ _____

What are you grateful for today?

_____

_____

What do you have plenty of?

_____

_____

What piece of wisdom are you grateful for?

_____

_____

Which current relationship are you grateful for?

_____

Saturday, November 17, 2018

In two words, how do you feel right now?

_____   _____

What are you grateful for today?

_____

_____

What freedoms are you taking for granted?

_____

_____

From where do you gain your sense of self-worth?

_____

_____

What good deed can you do in secret today?

_____

Sunday, November 18, 2018

In two words, how do you feel right now?

_____   _____

What are you grateful for today?

_____

_____

A goal you can accomplish today or get closer to:

_____

_____

What happened this week you want to remember:

_____

_____

How are you exactly the same as everyone else?

_____

Reflections

Note the highlights in your life in this moment.
Write down a quote that motivates you,
the titles of books you want to read
or documentaries to watch,
and a reason to smile
right now.

_____

_____

_____

_____

_____

_____

_____

_____

_____

Monday, November 19, 2018

In two words, how do you feel right now?

_____   _____

What are you grateful for today?

_____

_____

What are you looking forward to today?

_____

_____

A healthy habit you can start as of right now:

_____

_____

A friend you can send a letter to today:

_____

Tuesday, November 20, 2018

In two words, how do you feel right now?

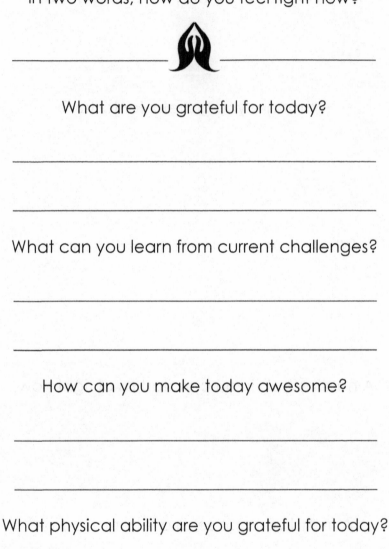

_____   _____

What are you grateful for today?

_____

_____

What can you learn from current challenges?

_____

_____

How can you make today awesome?

_____

_____

What physical ability are you grateful for today?

_____

Wednesday, November 21, 2018

In two words, how do you feel right now?

_____ _____

What are you grateful for today?

_____

_____

What would you like to do more often?

_____

_____

What would you like to do less often?

_____

_____

Modern technology you appreciate today:

_____

Thursday, November 22, 2018

In two words, how do you feel right now?

_____   _____

What are you grateful for today?

_____

_____

What can you do today to relax?

_____

_____

What is your priority today?

_____

_____

What skill are you most grateful for right now?

_____

Friday, November 23, 2018

In two words, how do you feel right now?

_____ _____

What are you grateful for today?

_____

_____

What do you have plenty of?

_____

_____

What piece of wisdom are you grateful for?

_____

_____

Which current relationship are you grateful for?

_____

Saturday, November 24, 2018

In two words, how do you feel right now?

_____

What are you grateful for today?

_____

_____

What freedoms are you taking for granted?

_____

_____

From where do you gain your sense of self-worth?

_____

_____

What good deed can you do in secret today?

_____

Sunday, November 25, 2018

In two words, how do you feel right now?

_____ _____

What are you grateful for today?

_____

_____

A goal you can accomplish today or get closer to:

_____

_____

What happened this week you want to remember:

_____

_____

How are you exactly the same as everyone else?

_____

Reflections

Note the highlights in your life in this moment.
Write down a quote that motivates you,
the titles of books you want to read
or documentaries to watch,
and a reason to smile
right now.

_____

_____

_____

_____

_____

_____

_____

_____

_____

Monday, November 26, 2018

In two words, how do you feel right now?

_____   _____

What are you grateful for today?

_____

_____

What are you looking forward to today?

_____

_____

A healthy habit you can start as of right now:

_____

_____

A friend you can send a letter to today:

_____

Tuesday, November 27, 2018

In two words, how do you feel right now?

_____   _____

What are you grateful for today?

_____

_____

What can you learn from current challenges?

_____

_____

How can you make today awesome?

_____

_____

What physical ability are you grateful for today?

_____

Wednesday, November 28, 2018

In two words, how do you feel right now?

_____ _____

What are you grateful for today?

_____

_____

What would you like to do more often?

_____

_____

What would you like to do less often?

_____

_____

Modern technology you appreciate today:

_____

Thursday, November 29, 2018

In two words, how do you feel right now?

_____   _____

What are you grateful for today?

_____

_____

What can you do today to relax?

_____

_____

What is your priority today?

_____

_____

What skill are you most grateful for right now?

_____

Friday, November 30, 2018

In two words, how do you feel right now?

_____ — _____

What are you grateful for today?

_____

_____

What do you have plenty of?

_____

_____

What piece of wisdom are you grateful for?

_____

_____

Which current relationship are you grateful for?

_____

Saturday, December 1, 2018

In two words, how do you feel right now?

_____   _____

What are you grateful for today?

_____

_____

What freedoms are you taking for granted?

_____

_____

From where do you gain your sense of self-worth?

_____

_____

What good deed can you do in secret today?

_____

December 1

Sunday, December 2, 2018

In two words, how do you feel right now?

_____   _____

What are you grateful for today?

_____

_____

A goal you can accomplish today or get closer to:

_____

_____

What happened this week you want to remember:

_____

_____

How are you exactly the same as everyone else?

_____

Reflections

Note the highlights in your life in this moment.
Write down a quote that motivates you,
the titles of books you want to read
or documentaries to watch,
and a reason to smile
right now.

_____

_____

_____

_____

_____

_____

_____

_____

Monday, December 3, 2018

In two words, how do you feel right now?

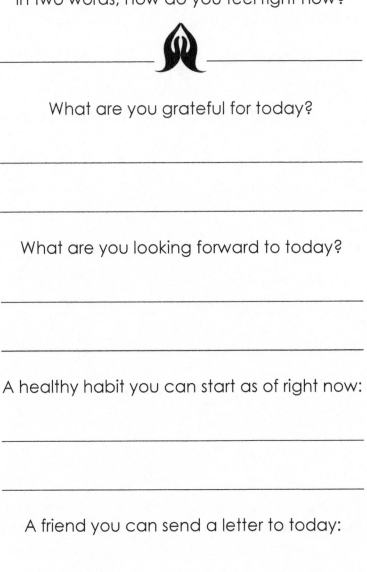

_____   _____

What are you grateful for today?

_____

_____

What are you looking forward to today?

_____

_____

A healthy habit you can start as of right now:

_____

_____

A friend you can send a letter to today:

_____

Tuesday, December 4, 2018

In two words, how do you feel right now?

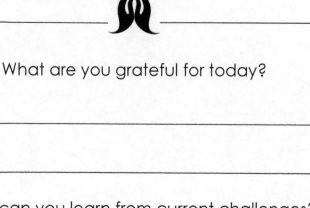

_____   _____

What are you grateful for today?

_____

_____

What can you learn from current challenges?

_____

_____

How can you make today awesome?

_____

_____

What physical ability are you grateful for today?

_____

Wednesday, December 5, 2018

In two words, how do you feel right now?

_____ _____

What are you grateful for today?

_____

_____

What would you like to do more often?

_____

_____

What would you like to do less often?

_____

_____

Modern technology you appreciate today:

_____

Thursday, December 6, 2018

In two words, how do you feel right now?

_____   _____

What are you grateful for today?

_____

_____

What can you do today to relax?

_____

_____

What is your priority today?

_____

_____

What skill are you most grateful for right now?

_____

Friday, December 7, 2018

In two words, how do you feel right now?

_____   _____

What are you grateful for today?

_____

_____

What do you have plenty of?

_____

_____

What piece of wisdom are you grateful for?

_____

_____

Which current relationship are you grateful for?

_____

Saturday, December 8, 2018

In two words, how do you feel right now?

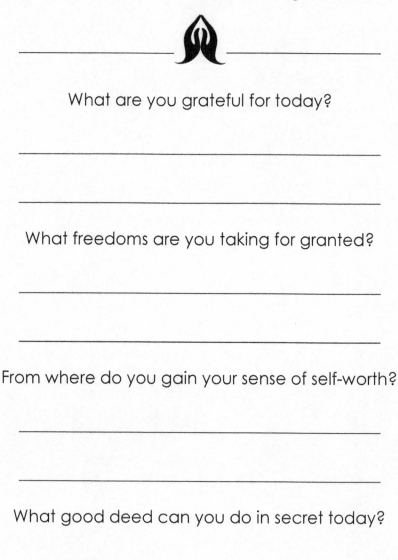

_____   _____

What are you grateful for today?

_____

_____

What freedoms are you taking for granted?

_____

_____

From where do you gain your sense of self-worth?

_____

_____

What good deed can you do in secret today?

_____

Sunday, December 9, 2018

In two words, how do you feel right now?

_____ _____

What are you grateful for today?

_____

_____

A goal you can accomplish today or get closer to:

_____

_____

What happened this week you want to remember:

_____

_____

How are you exactly the same as everyone else?

_____

Reflections

Note the highlights in your life in this moment.
Write down a quote that motivates you,
the titles of books you want to read
or documentaries to watch,
and a reason to smile
right now.

_____

_____

_____

_____

_____

_____

_____

_____

Monday, December 10, 2018

In two words, how do you feel right now?

_____   _____

What are you grateful for today?

_____

_____

What are you looking forward to today?

_____

_____

A healthy habit you can start as of right now:

_____

_____

A friend you can send a letter to today:

_____

Tuesday, December 11, 2018

In two words, how do you feel right now?

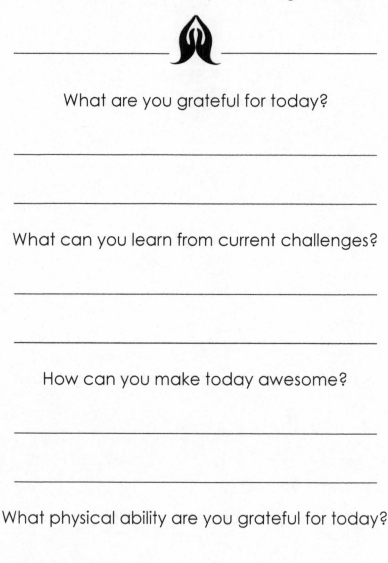

_____   _____

What are you grateful for today?

_____

_____

What can you learn from current challenges?

_____

_____

How can you make today awesome?

_____

_____

What physical ability are you grateful for today?

_____

December 11

Wednesday, December 12, 2018

In two words, how do you feel right now?

_____ — _____

What are you grateful for today?

_____

_____

What would you like to do more often?

_____

_____

What would you like to do less often?

_____

_____

Modern technology you appreciate today:

_____

Thursday, December 13, 2018

In two words, how do you feel right now?

_____ _____

What are you grateful for today?

_____

_____

What can you do today to relax?

_____

_____

What is your priority today?

_____

_____

What skill are you most grateful for right now?

_____

December 13

Friday, December 14, 2018

In two words, how do you feel right now?

_____ — _____

What are you grateful for today?

_____

_____

What do you have plenty of?

_____

_____

What piece of wisdom are you grateful for?

_____

_____

Which current relationship are you grateful for?

_____

Saturday, December 15, 2018

In two words, how do you feel right now?

_____ — _____

What are you grateful for today?

_____

_____

What freedoms are you taking for granted?

_____

_____

From where do you gain your sense of self-worth?

_____

_____

What good deed can you do in secret today?

_____

Sunday, December 16, 2018

In two words, how do you feel right now?

_____   _____

What are you grateful for today?

_____

_____

A goal you can accomplish today or get closer to:

_____

_____

What happened this week you want to remember:

_____

_____

How are you exactly the same as everyone else?

_____

Reflections

Note the highlights in your life in this moment.
Write down a quote that motivates you,
the titles of books you want to read
or documentaries to watch,
and a reason to smile
right now.

_____

_____

_____

_____

_____

_____

_____

_____

_____

Monday, December 17, 2018

In two words, how do you feel right now?

_____   _____

What are you grateful for today?

_____

_____

What are you looking forward to today?

_____

_____

A healthy habit you can start as of right now:

_____

_____

A friend you can send a letter to today:

_____

Tuesday, December 18, 2018

In two words, how do you feel right now?

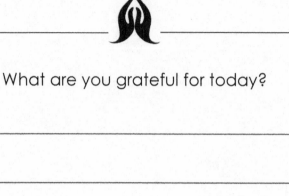

_____   _____

What are you grateful for today?

_____

_____

What can you learn from current challenges?

_____

_____

How can you make today awesome?

_____

_____

What physical ability are you grateful for today?

_____

Wednesday, December 19, 2018

In two words, how do you feel right now?

_____   _____

What are you grateful for today?

_____

_____

What would you like to do more often?

_____

_____

What would you like to do less often?

_____

_____

Modern technology you appreciate today:

_____

Thursday, December 20, 2018

In two words, how do you feel right now?

_____ _____

What are you grateful for today?

_____

_____

What can you do today to relax?

_____

_____

What is your priority today?

_____

_____

What skill are you most grateful for right now?

_____

December 20

Friday, December 21, 2018

In two words, how do you feel right now?

_____   _____

What are you grateful for today?

_____

_____

What do you have plenty of?

_____

_____

What piece of wisdom are you grateful for?

_____

_____

Which current relationship are you grateful for?

_____

Saturday, December 22, 2018

In two words, how do you feel right now?

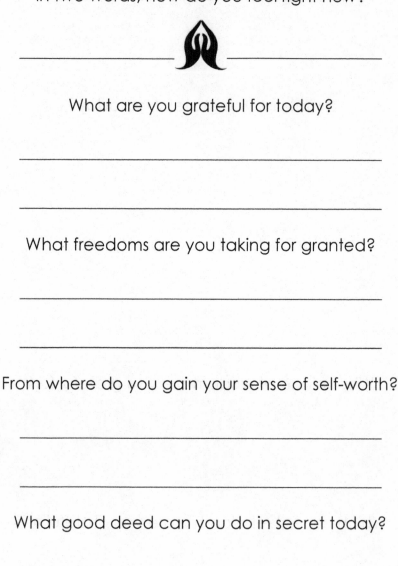

_____   _____

What are you grateful for today?

_____

_____

What freedoms are you taking for granted?

_____

_____

From where do you gain your sense of self-worth?

_____

_____

What good deed can you do in secret today?

_____

Sunday, December 23, 2018

In two words, how do you feel right now?

_____   _____

What are you grateful for today?

_____

_____

A goal you can accomplish today or get closer to:

_____

_____

What happened this week you want to remember:

_____

_____

How are you exactly the same as everyone else?

_____

Reflections

Note the highlights in your life in this moment.
Write down a quote that motivates you,
the titles of books you want to read
or documentaries to watch,
and a reason to smile
right now.

_____

_____

_____

_____

_____

_____

_____

_____

_____

Monday, December 24, 2018

In two words, how do you feel right now?

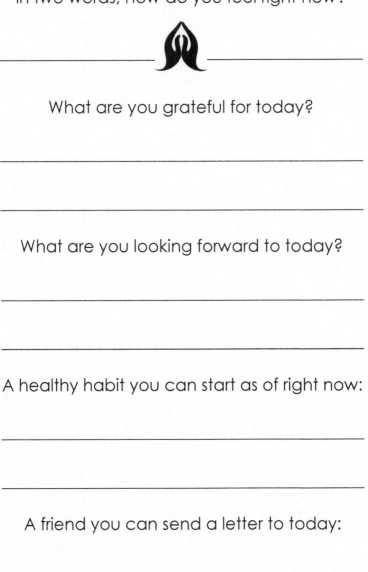

_____   _____

What are you grateful for today?

_____

_____

What are you looking forward to today?

_____

_____

A healthy habit you can start as of right now:

_____

_____

A friend you can send a letter to today:

_____

Tuesday, December 25, 2018

In two words, how do you feel right now?

_____

What are you grateful for today?

_____

_____

What can you learn from current challenges?

_____

_____

How can you make today awesome?

_____

_____

What physical ability are you grateful for today?

_____

December 25

Wednesday, December 26, 2018

In two words, how do you feel right now?

_____ _____

What are you grateful for today?

_____

_____

What would you like to do more often?

_____

_____

What would you like to do less often?

_____

_____

Modern technology you appreciate today:

_____

Thursday, December 27, 2018

In two words, how do you feel right now?

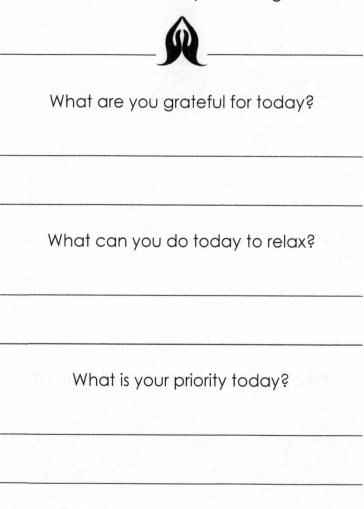

_____   _____

What are you grateful for today?

_____

_____

What can you do today to relax?

_____

_____

What is your priority today?

_____

_____

What skill are you most grateful for right now?

_____

December 27

Friday, December 28, 2018

In two words, how do you feel right now?

_____ — 🙏 — _____

What are you grateful for today?

_____

_____

What do you have plenty of?

_____

_____

What piece of wisdom are you grateful for?

_____

_____

Which current relationship are you grateful for?

_____

Saturday, December 29, 2018

In two words, how do you feel right now?

_____   _____

What are you grateful for today?

_____

_____

What freedoms are you taking for granted?

_____

_____

From where do you gain your sense of self-worth?

_____

_____

What good deed can you do in secret today?

_____

Sunday, December 30, 2018

In two words, how do you feel right now?

_____   _____

What are you grateful for today?

_____

_____

A goal you can accomplish today or get closer to:

_____

_____

What happened this week you want to remember:

_____

_____

How are you exactly the same as everyone else?

_____

Reflections

List anything from the past year you do not want to carry with you into 2019 (be it grudges, outdated opinions, judgments, or beliefs that no longer serve your evolution). Then write down your intentions for 2019. Get next year's Mahalo Gratitude Journal from BuddhistBootCamp.com

_____

_____

_____

_____

_____

_____

_____

_____

Monday, December 31, 2018

In two words, how do you feel right now?

_____   _____

What are you grateful for today?

_____

_____

What are you looking forward to today?

_____

_____

A healthy habit you can start as of right now:

_____

_____

A friend you can send a letter to today:

_____

Core Values

"Happiness is when what you think,
what you say, and what you do
are all in alignment."
— Gandhi

Write down your core values and a paragraph describing the kind of life you want to lead, then cross-reference it with the life you're currently living, and you will see where you have some work to do.

Live a congruent life.
Say what you mean, and mean what you say.

_____

_____

_____

_____

_____

_____

_____

_____

_____

_____

_____

_____

SIT HAPPENS
Buddhist Boot Camp

ALSO BY TIMBER HAWKEYE:

BUDDHIST BOOT CAMP

A collection of inspirational journal entries and letters
he sent to friends over the course of eight years.
Each chapter is only a page long and
you can read them in any order.

and

FAITHFULLY RELIGIONLESS

A memoir inviting you to discover the difference
between feelings and emotions, the disparity
between truths and facts, and the
countless benefits of mindful living.

Timber Hawkeye is the bestselling author of
Buddhist Boot Camp and **Faithfully Religionless**.

He offers a secular approach to being at peace
with the world (both within and around us), with
the intention to awaken, enlighten,
enrich and inspire.

For additional information about Timber and his
books or podcast, and to watch his TED Talk
about gratitude, please visit

BuddhistBootCamp.com

Also on Facebook.com/BuddhistBootCamp
and on Instagram @BuddhistBootCamp

CPSIA information can be obtained
at www.ICGtesting.com
Printed in the USA
BVOW08*0506101117
500033BV00003BB/3/P